Staatsgrenze
1981 – 1983

Seiichi Furuya

玉

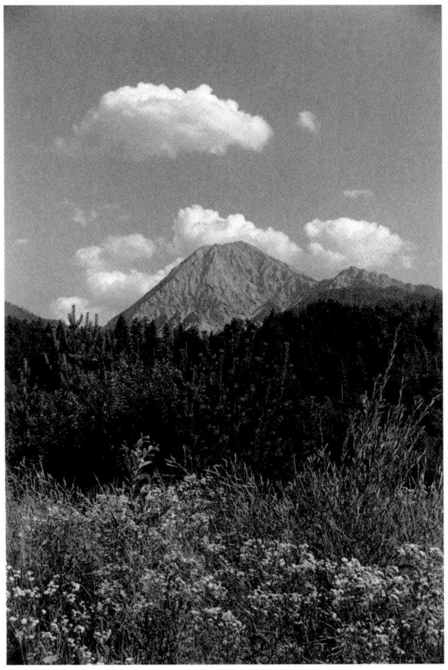

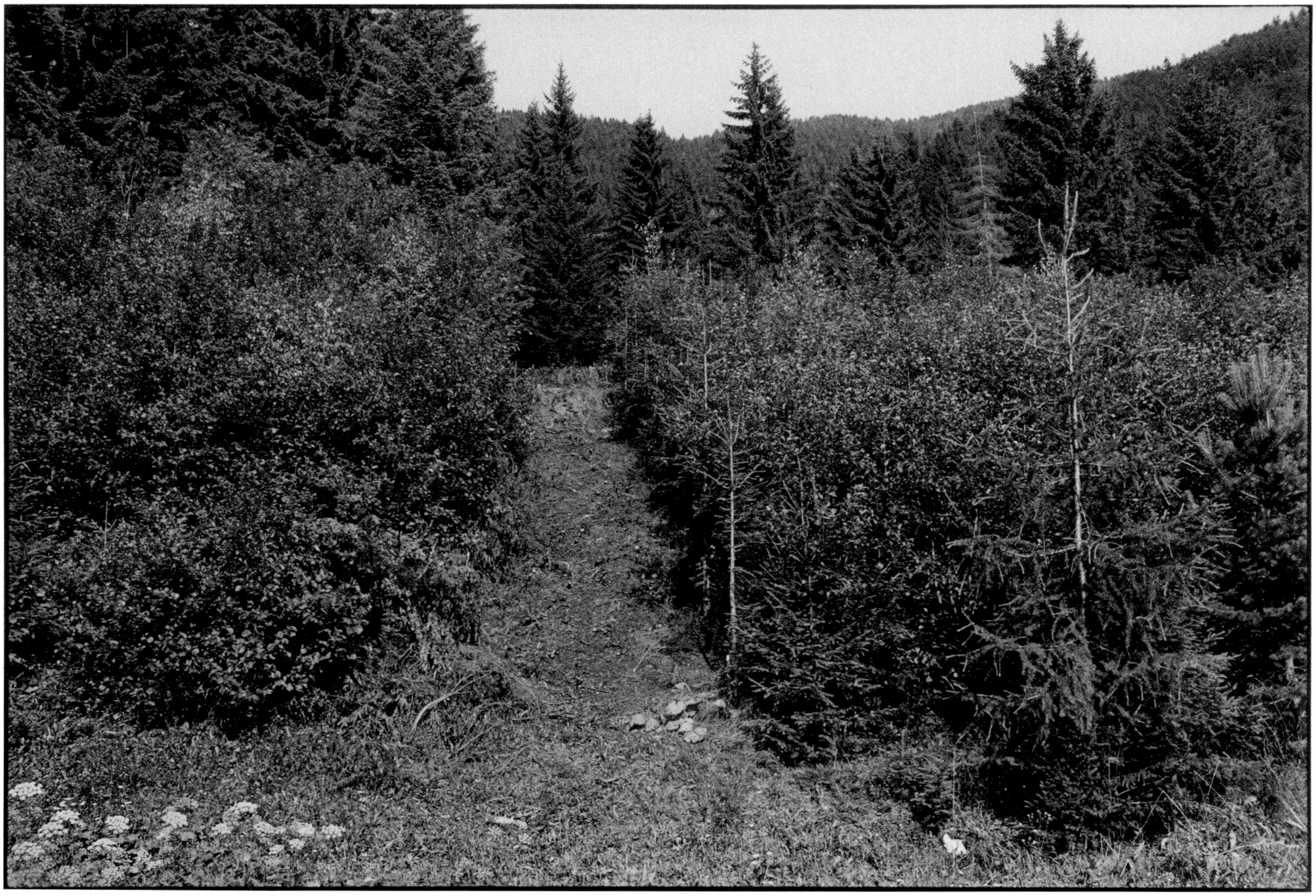

Im Juli 1983 wurden vier illegale türkische Grenzgänger von jugoslawischen Grenzbeamten beschossen. Ein Türke wurde dabei verletzt. Zur Zeit versuchen viele Türken über die ›grüne Grenze‹ durch Österreich nach Deutschland zu gelangen.

Wurzenpass, 1983

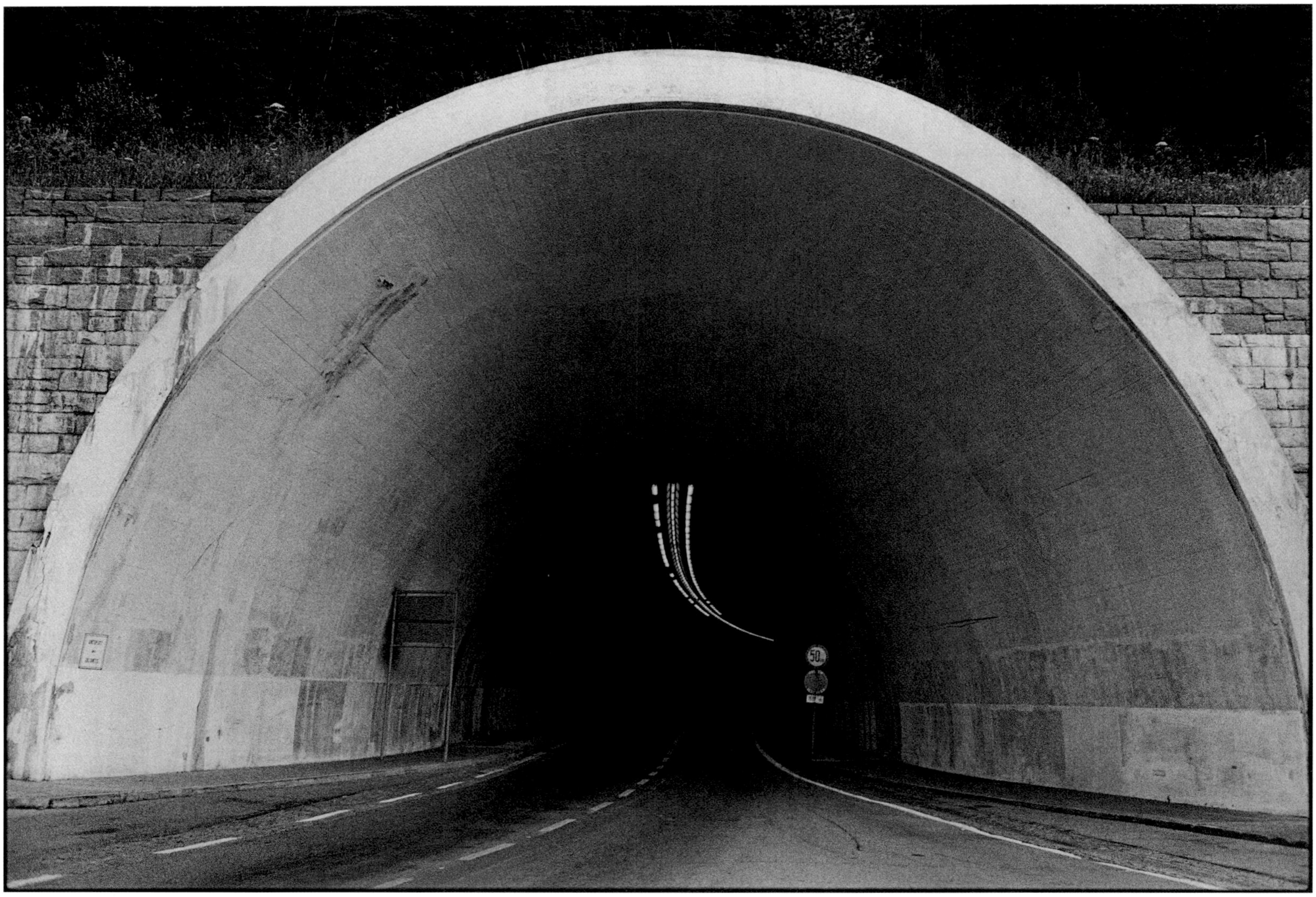

»IN DER ZEIT DER NATIONALSOZIALISTISCHEN GEWALTHERRSCHAFT HABEN EINIGE TAUSEND HÄFTLINGE DES KONZENTRATIONSLAGERS MAUTHAUSEN – IN IHRER MEHRZAHL FRANZOSEN – IN DEN JAHREN 1943 BIS 1945 AN DER ERRICHTUNG DES LOIBLTUNNELS GEARBEITET. VON DENEN VIELE BEI DER GRAUSAMEN ZWANGSARBEIT DEN TOD FANDEN.«
(aus einer Gedenkstein-Inschrift)

Loiblpass, 1983

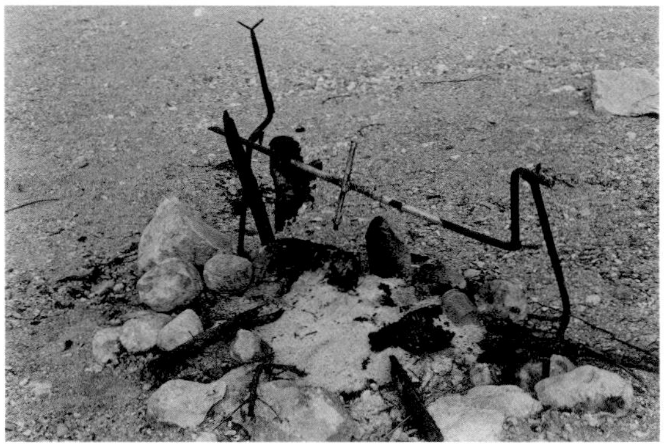

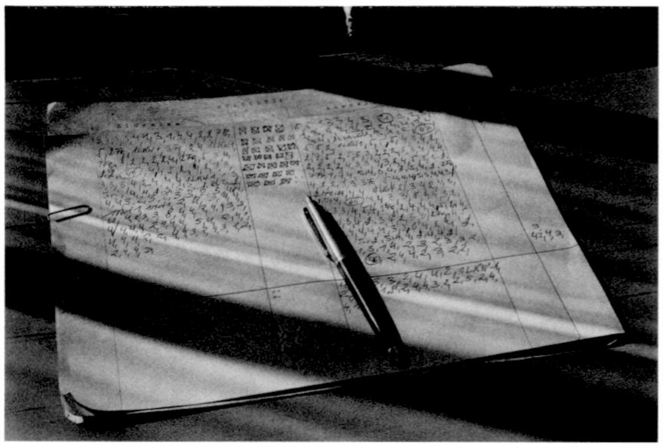

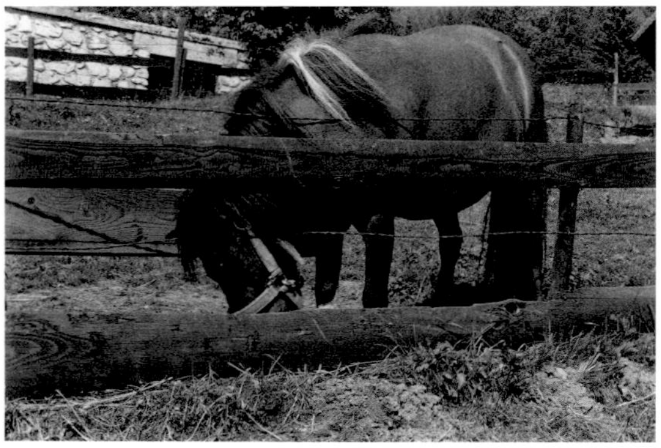

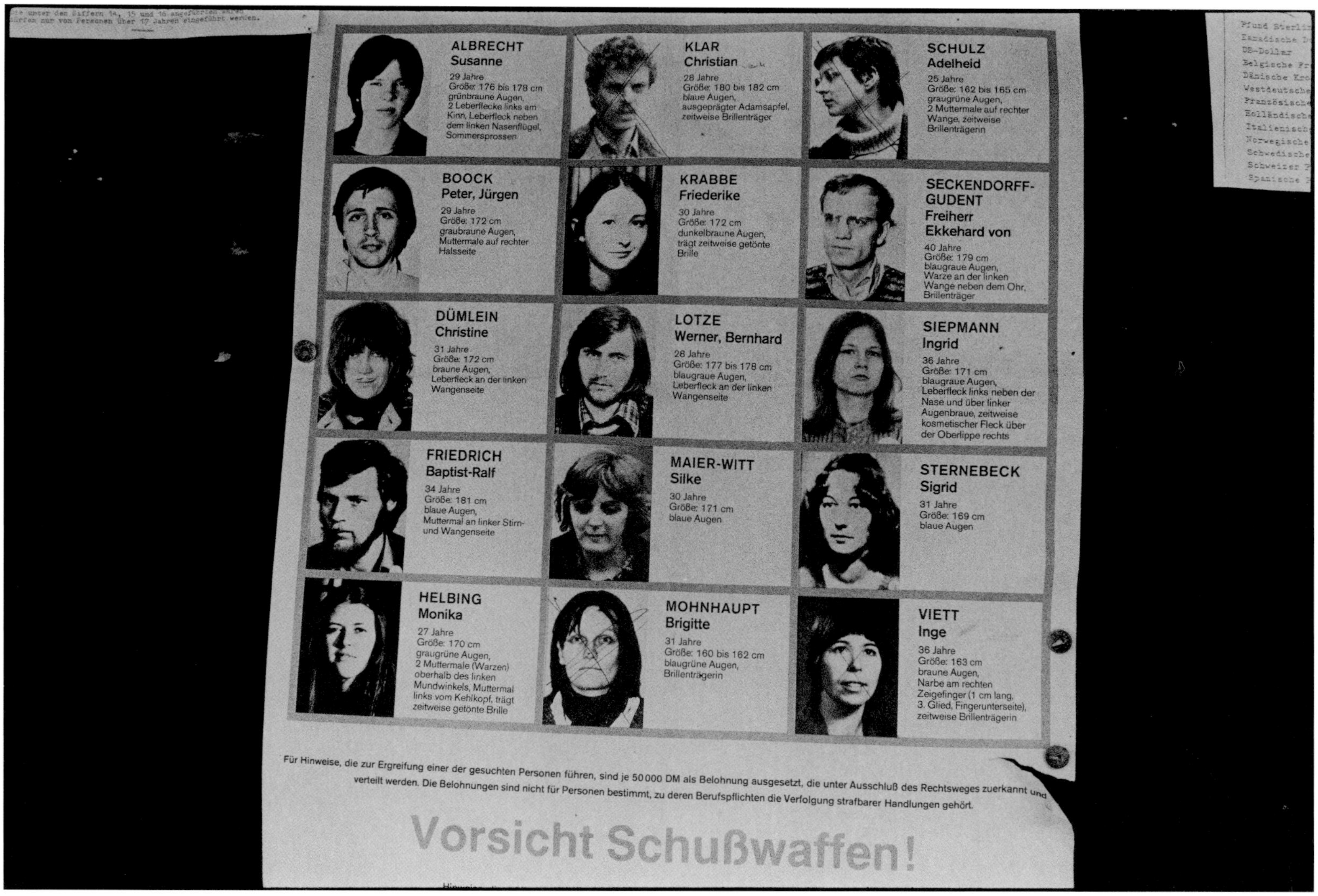

Fahndungsplakat nach RAF-Terroristen

Seebergsattel, 1983

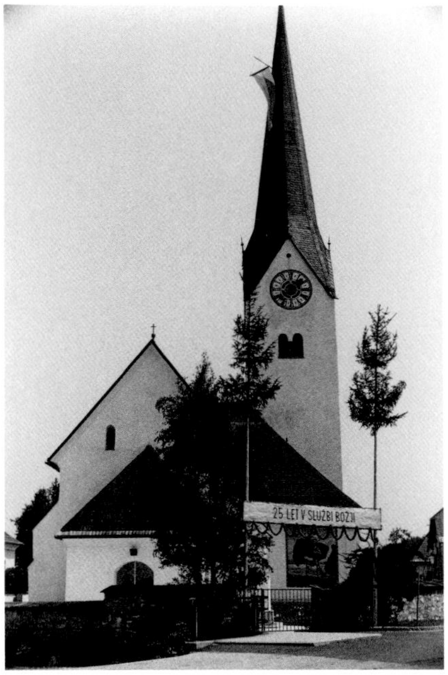
25 LET V SLUŽBI BOŽJI

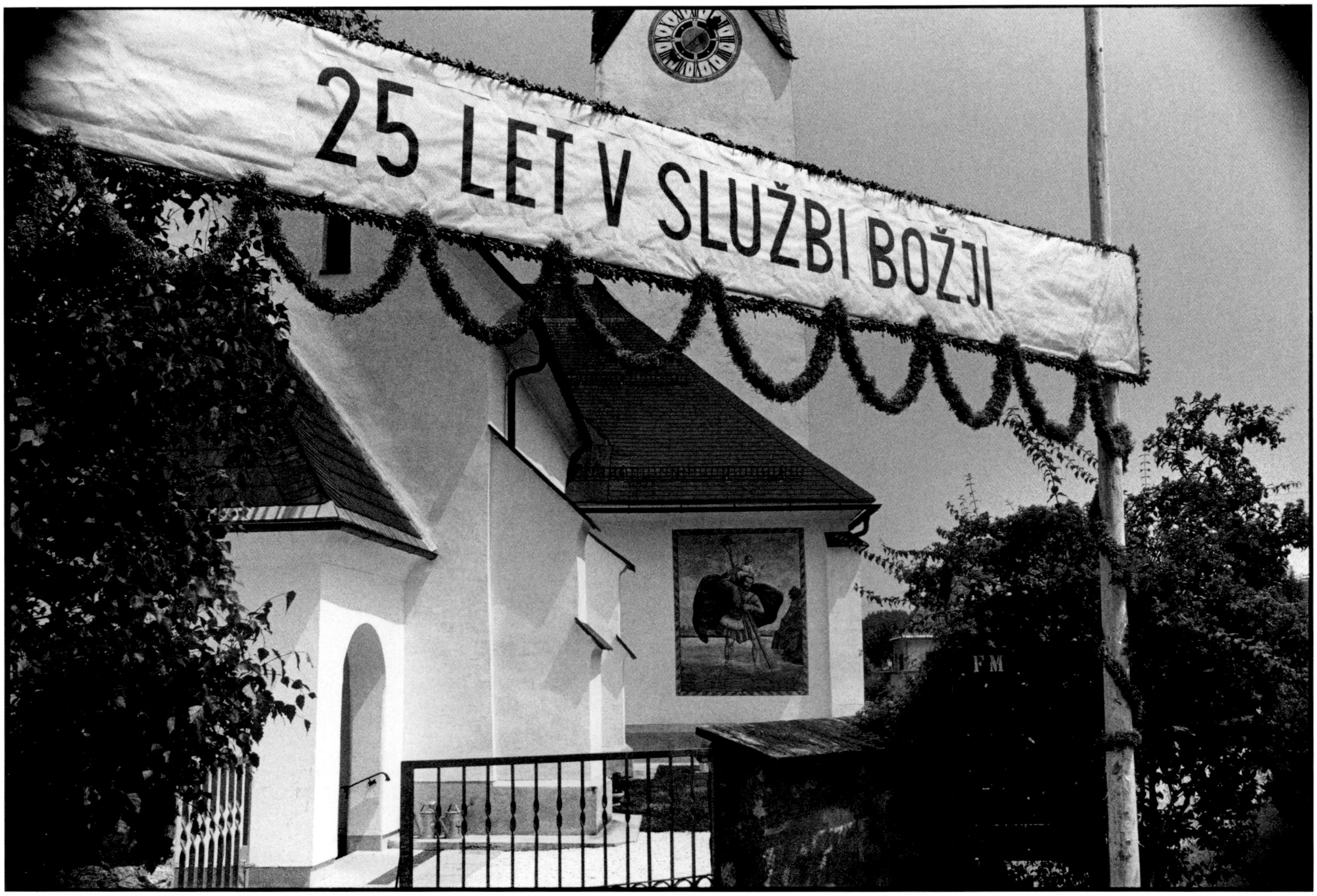

»Auf dem Transparent steht: ›25 Jahre im Dienste Gottes‹ auf Slowenisch, denn in dieser Gemeinde versteht man das besser.«
Globasnitz / Globasnica, 1983

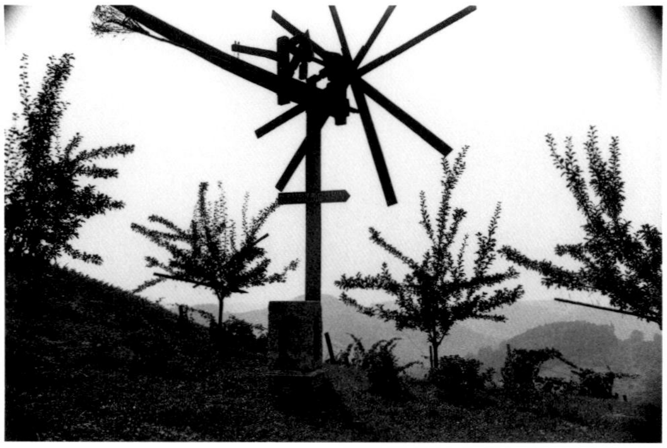

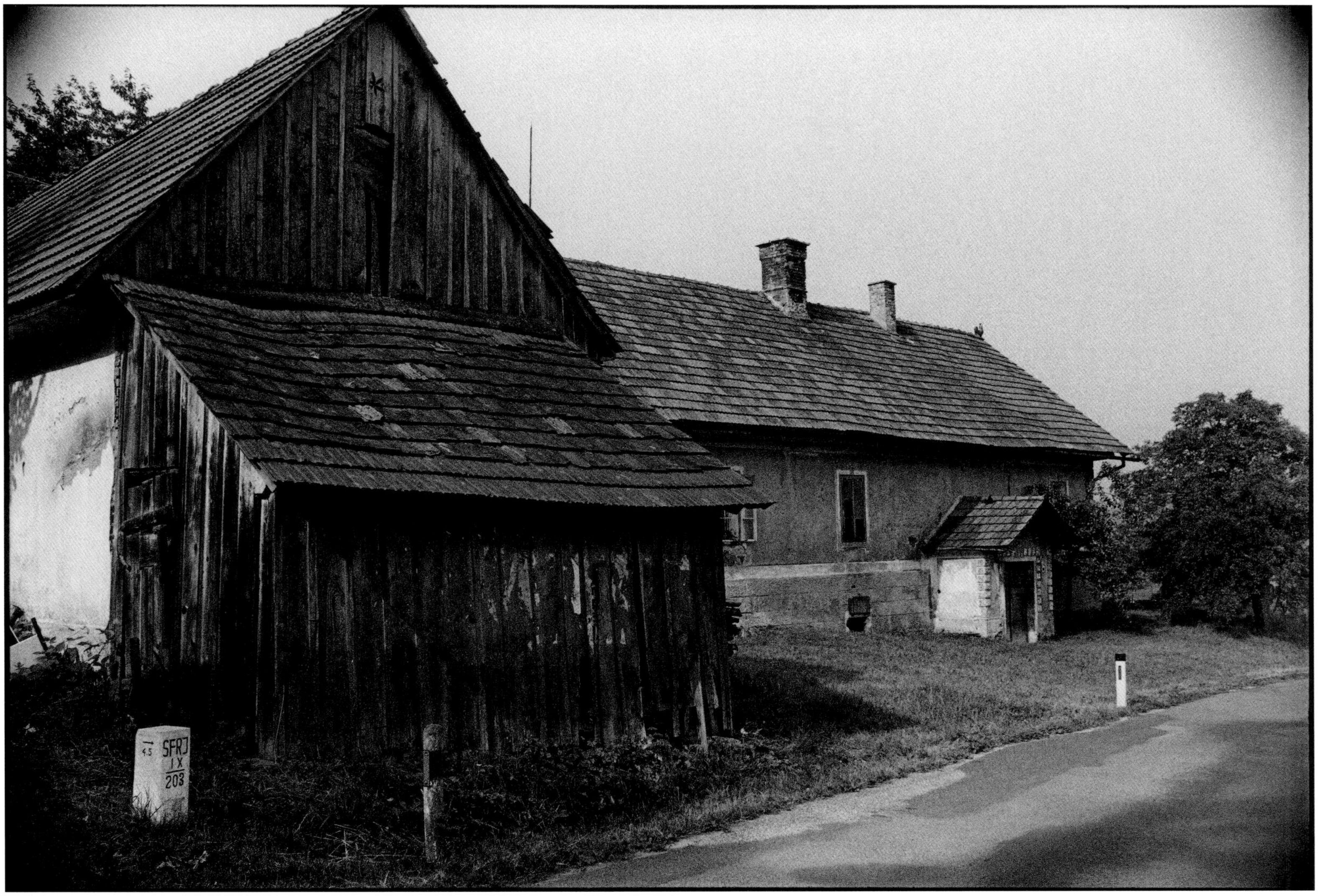

»Um Gottes Willen, bleiben Sie draußen! Hier ist Jugoslawien. Wenn die Soldaten vorbeikommen, nehmen sie Sie mit!«

Südsteirische Weinstraße, 1983

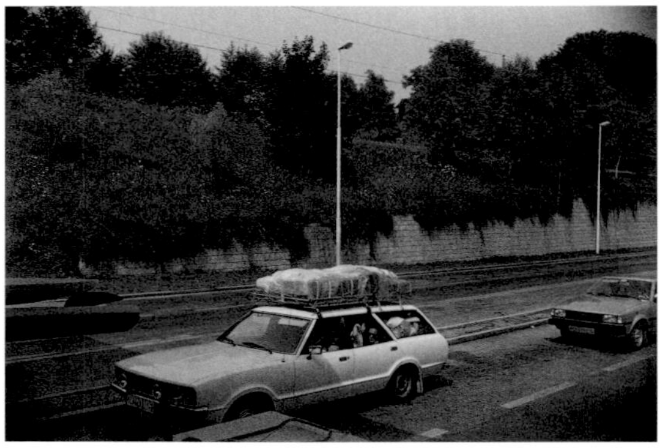

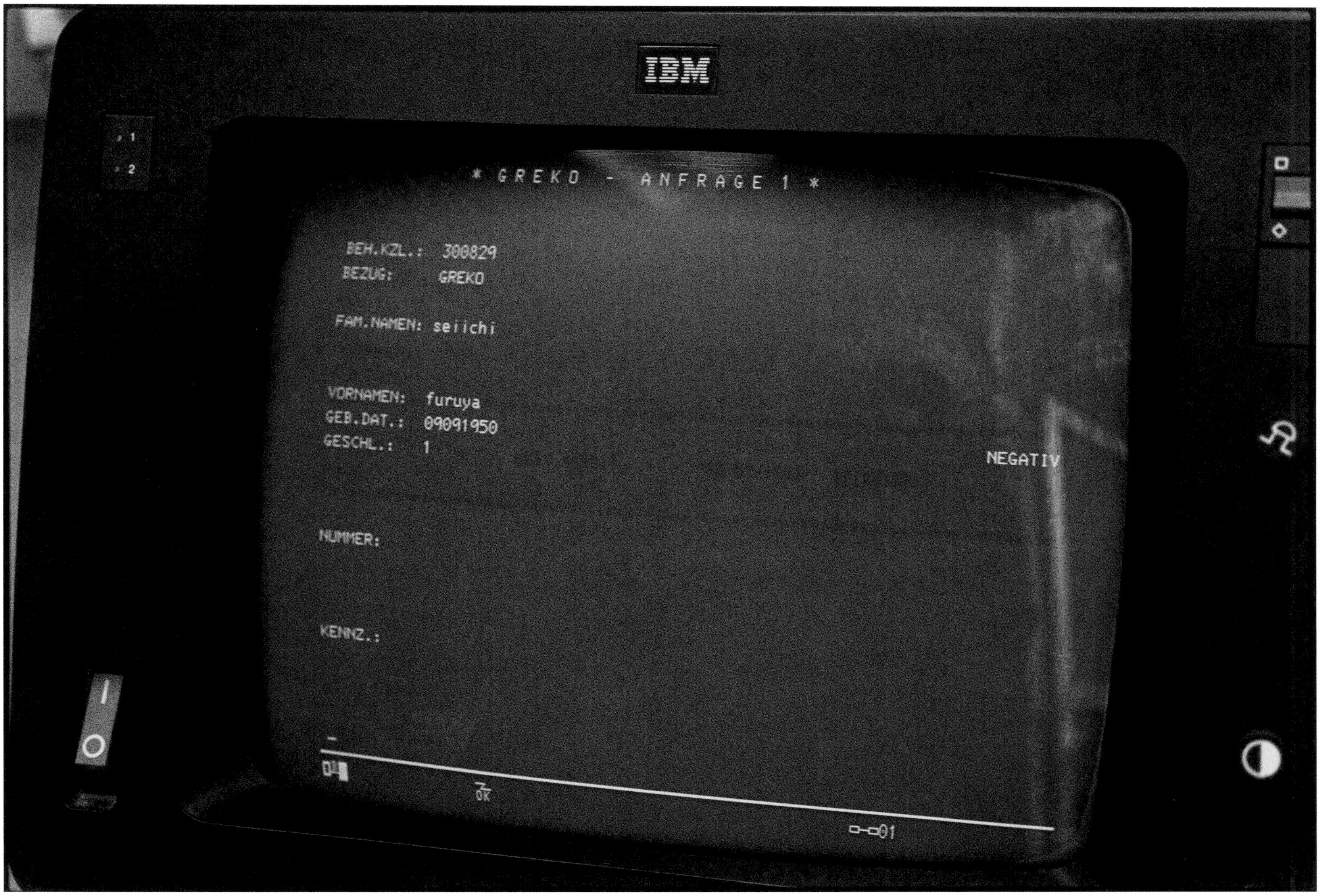

Greko-Anfrage
Spielfeld, 1983

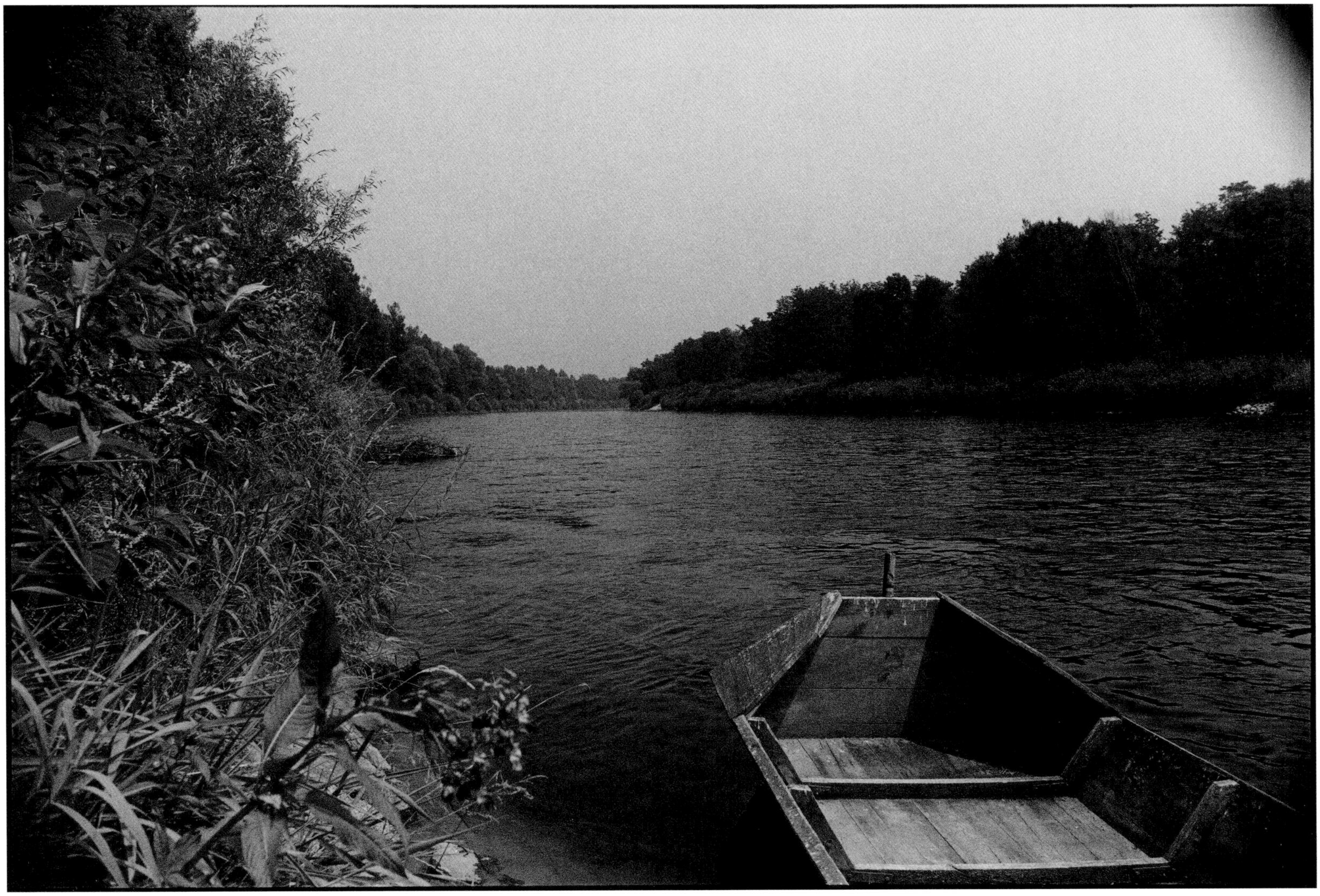

Die schlechte Versorgungslage in Jugoslawien ließ einen Wiener Schmugglerring aktiv werden. Anfang 1983 kenterte in der Mur bei Bad Radkersburg ein mit 300 kg gemahlenem Schmuggel-Kaffee beladenes Schlauchboot.

Radkersburg, 1983

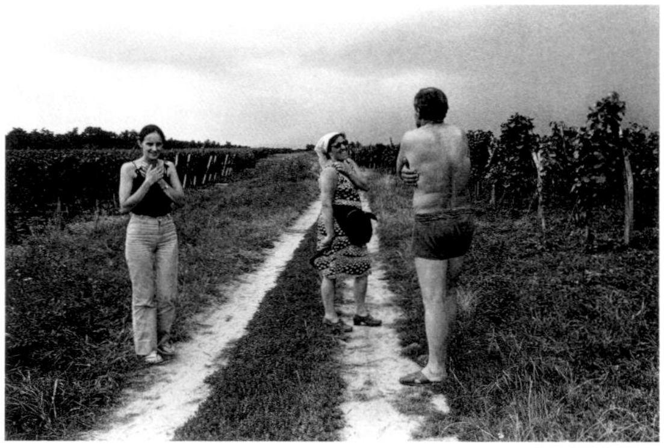

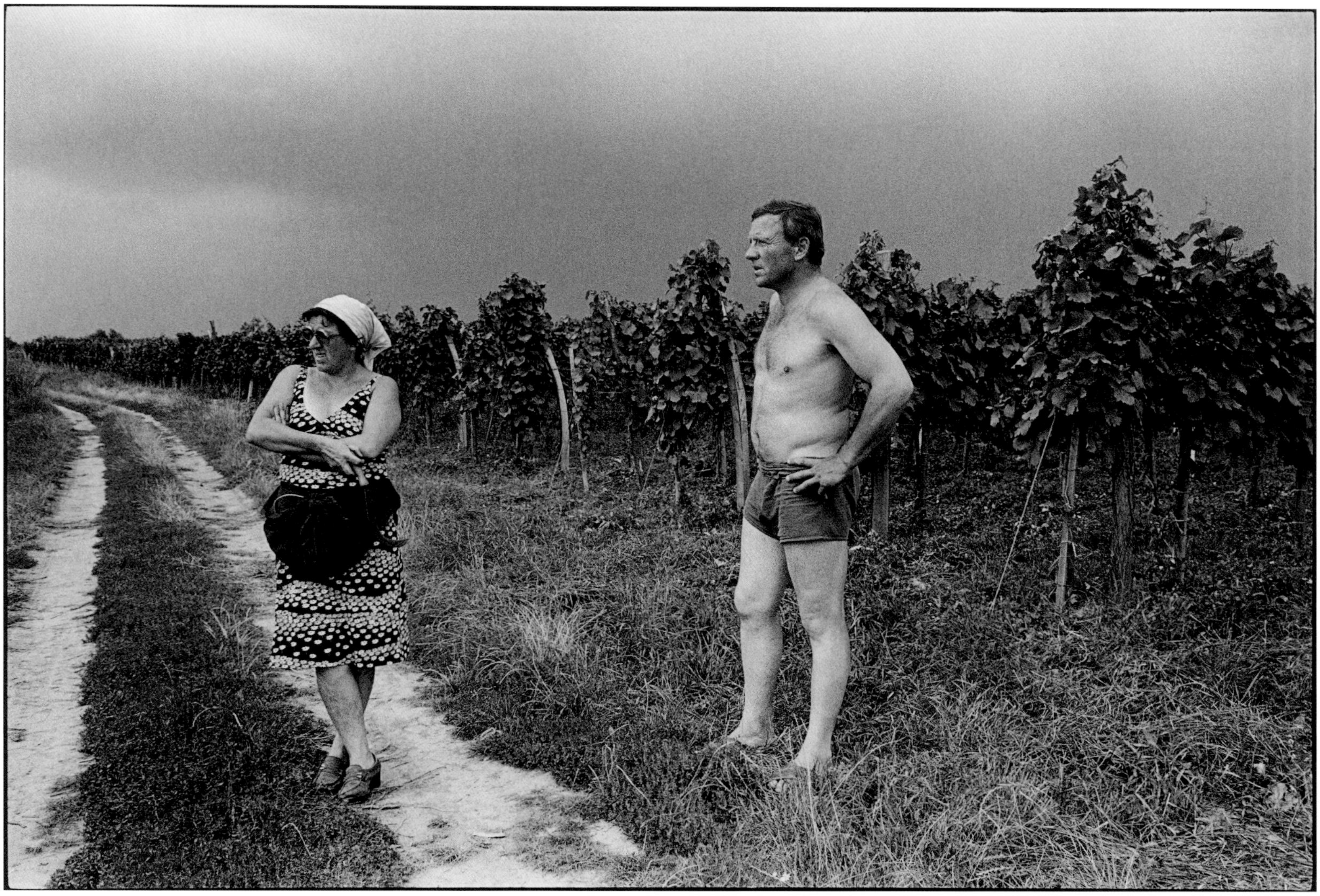

»Wenn Sie dreimal laut schreien, dann komme ich Ihnen zu Hilfe.«

Rattersdorf, 1981

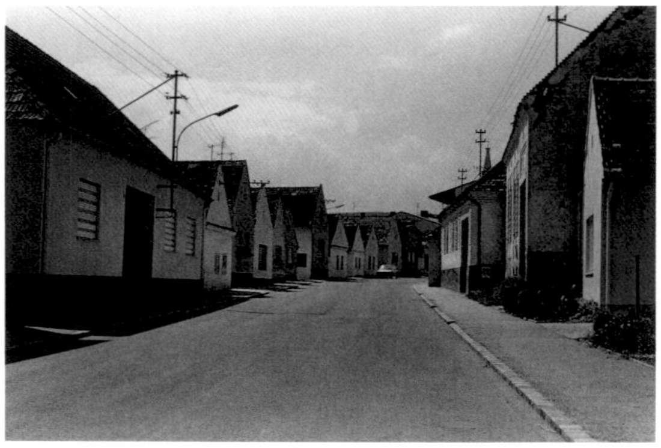

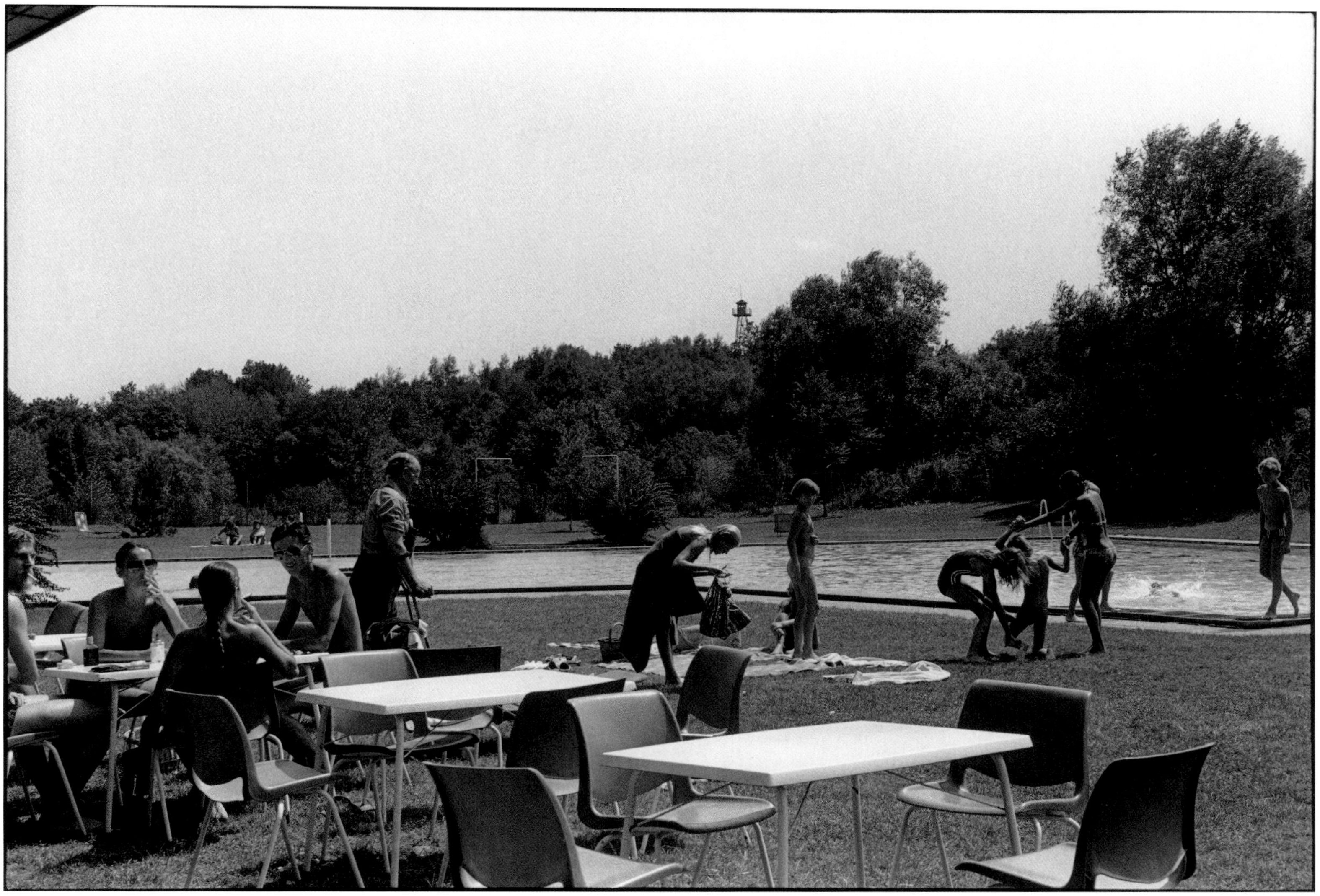

»Bei Badewetter richtet der ungarische Grenzsoldat sein Fernrohr für lange Zeit nur auf unsere Liegewiese.«

Loipersbach im Burgenland, 1981

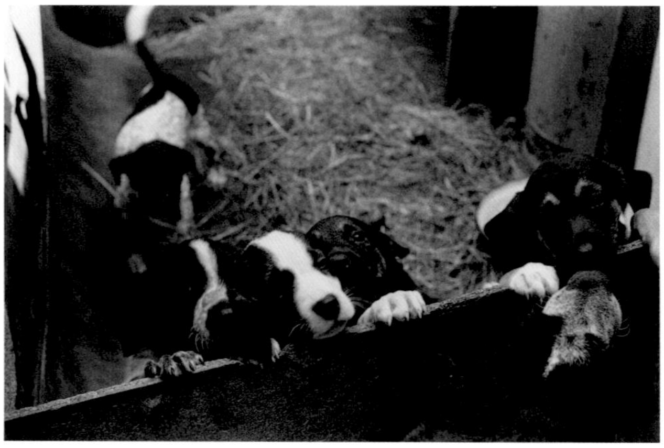

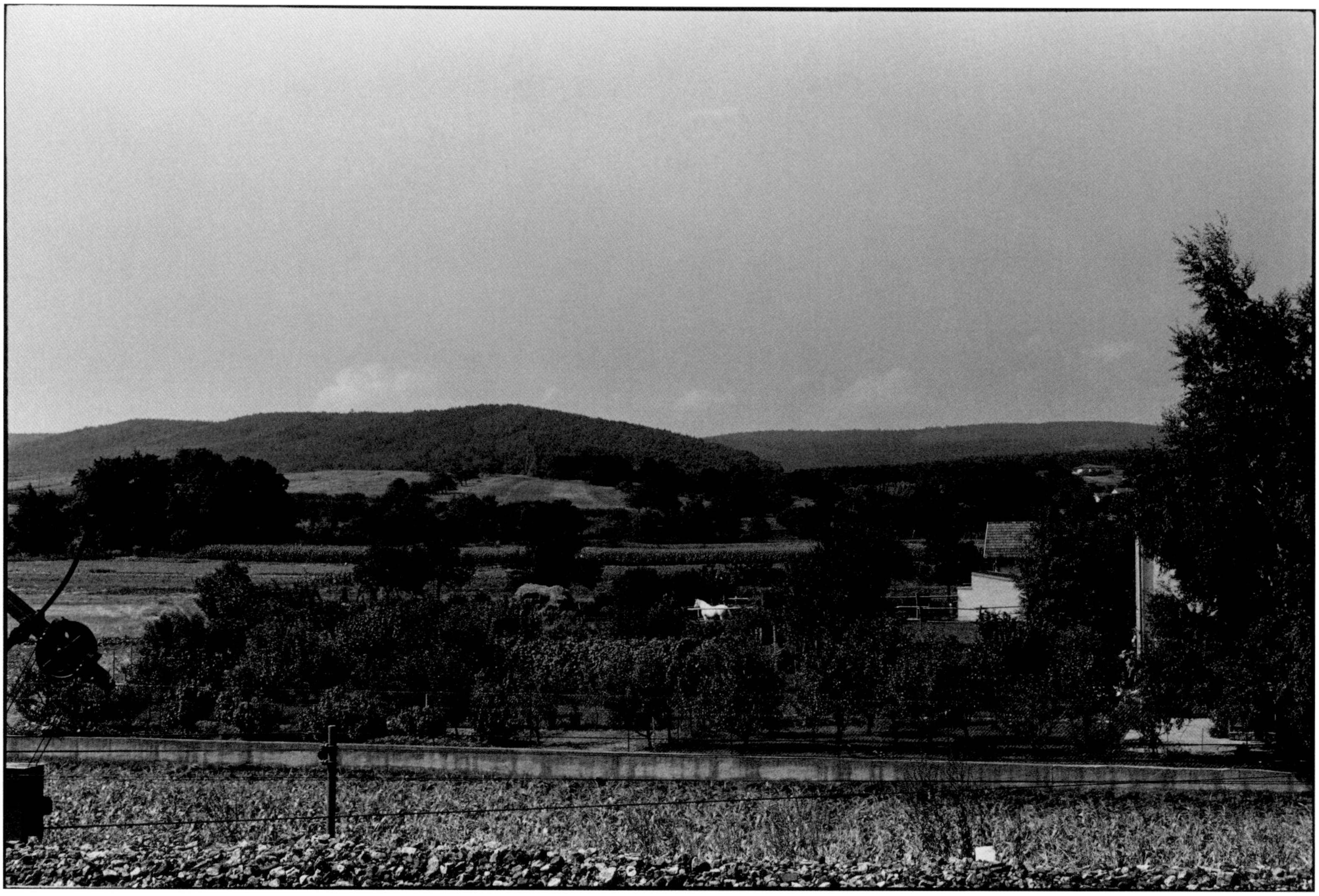

»Auf dieser Bahnlinie flüchten manchmal Leute aus dem Osten nach Österreich. Vor vier Jahren ist ein Mädchen aus Ostdeutschland illegal über die Grenze, um nach Westdeutschland zu gelangen.«

Loipersbach im Burgenland, 1981

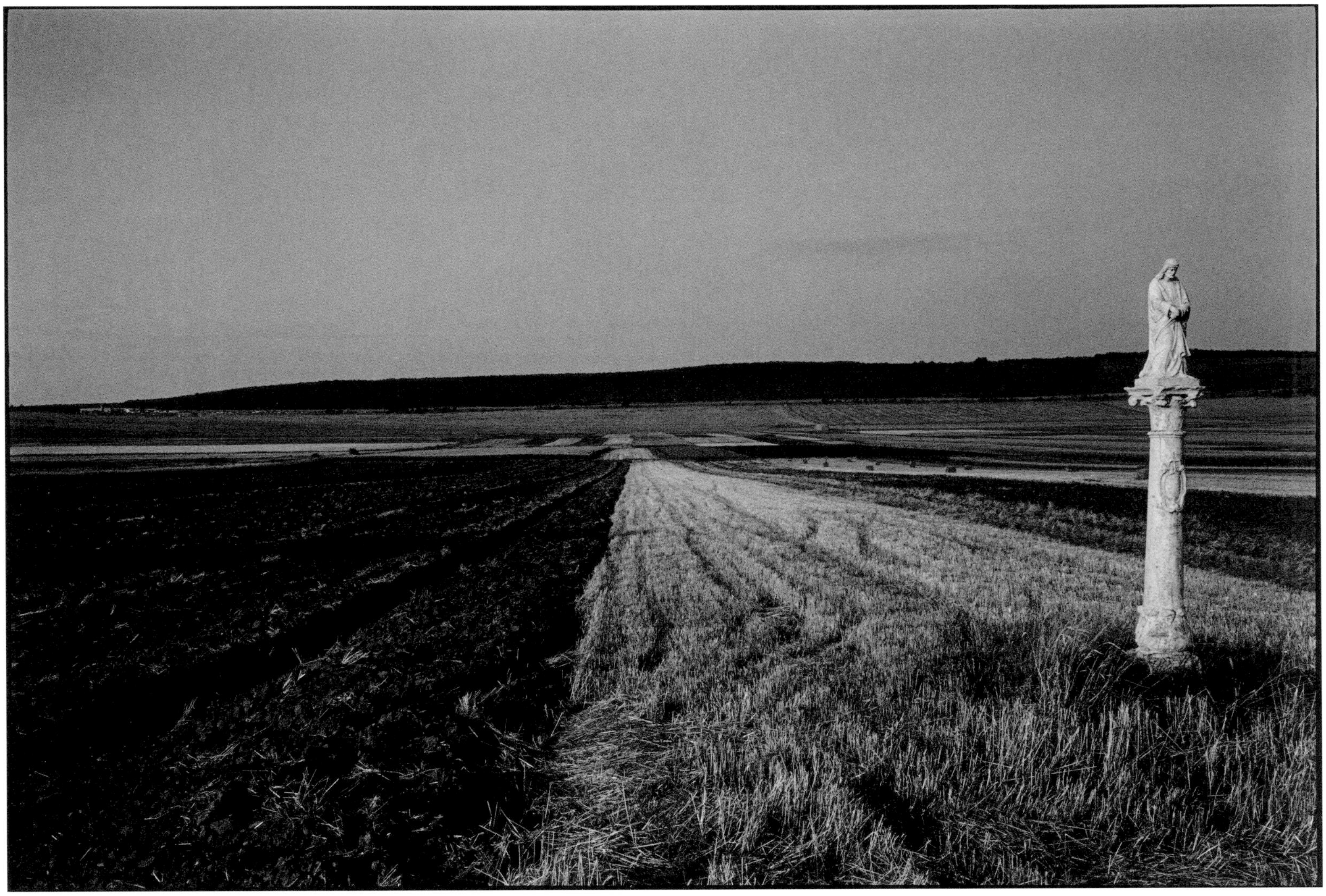

»Hier ist die freie westliche Welt zu Ende und fängt erst in Japan wieder an. Wenn in der Nacht das Wild über den Grenzstreifen geht, gehen Leuchtminen auf und die ungarischen Soldaten marschieren auf.«

Schattendorf, 1981

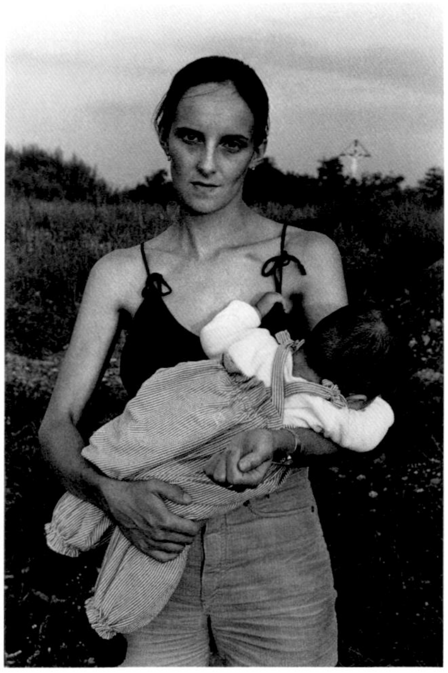

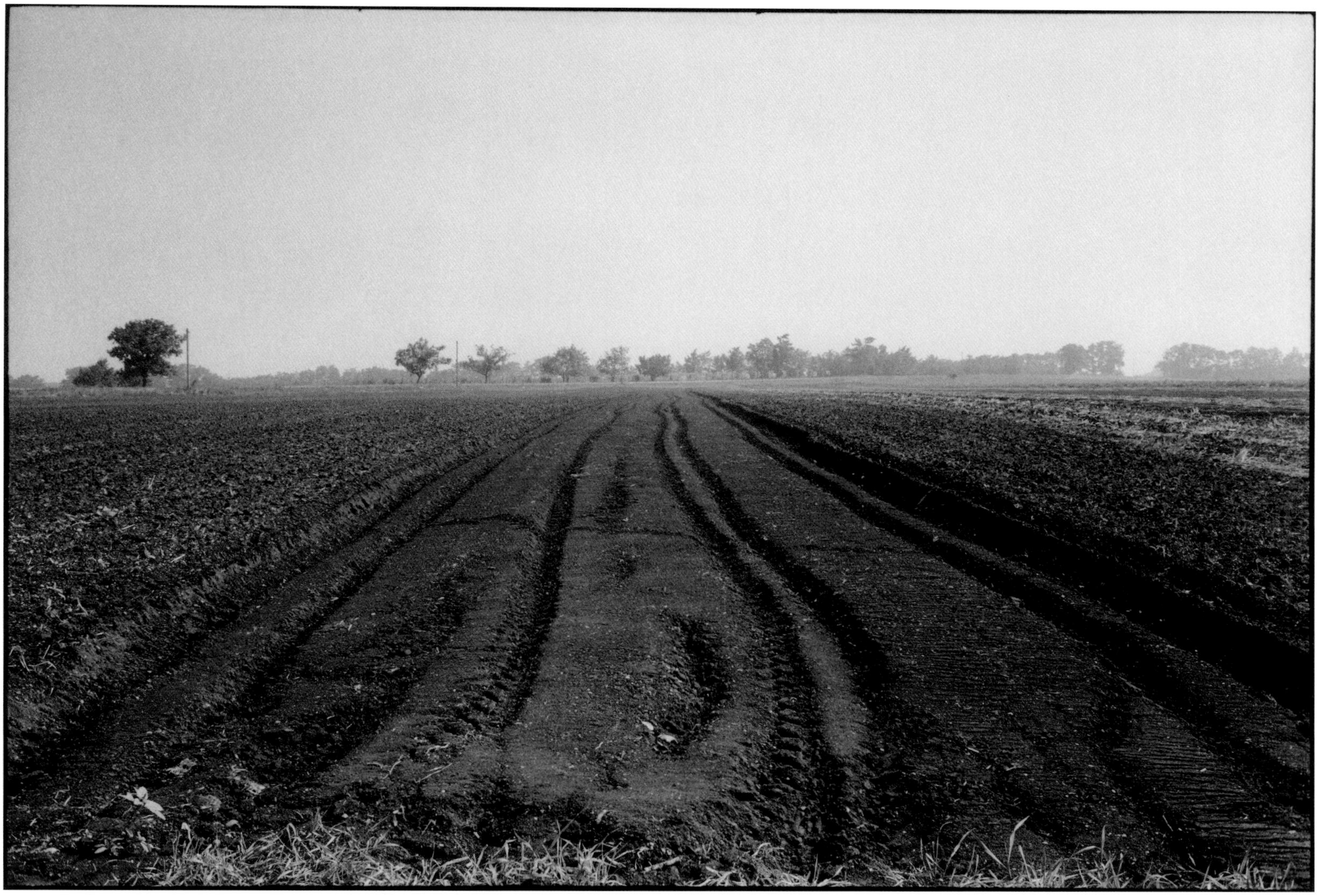

»Hier ist das ungarische Jagdflugzeug MiG-21 abgestürzt. Die Ungarn haben bald darauf alle Flugzeugtrümmer und den Piloten abgeholt.«

Andau, 1981

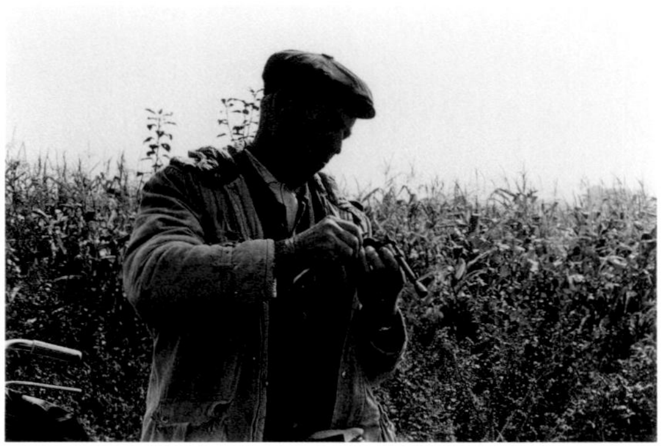

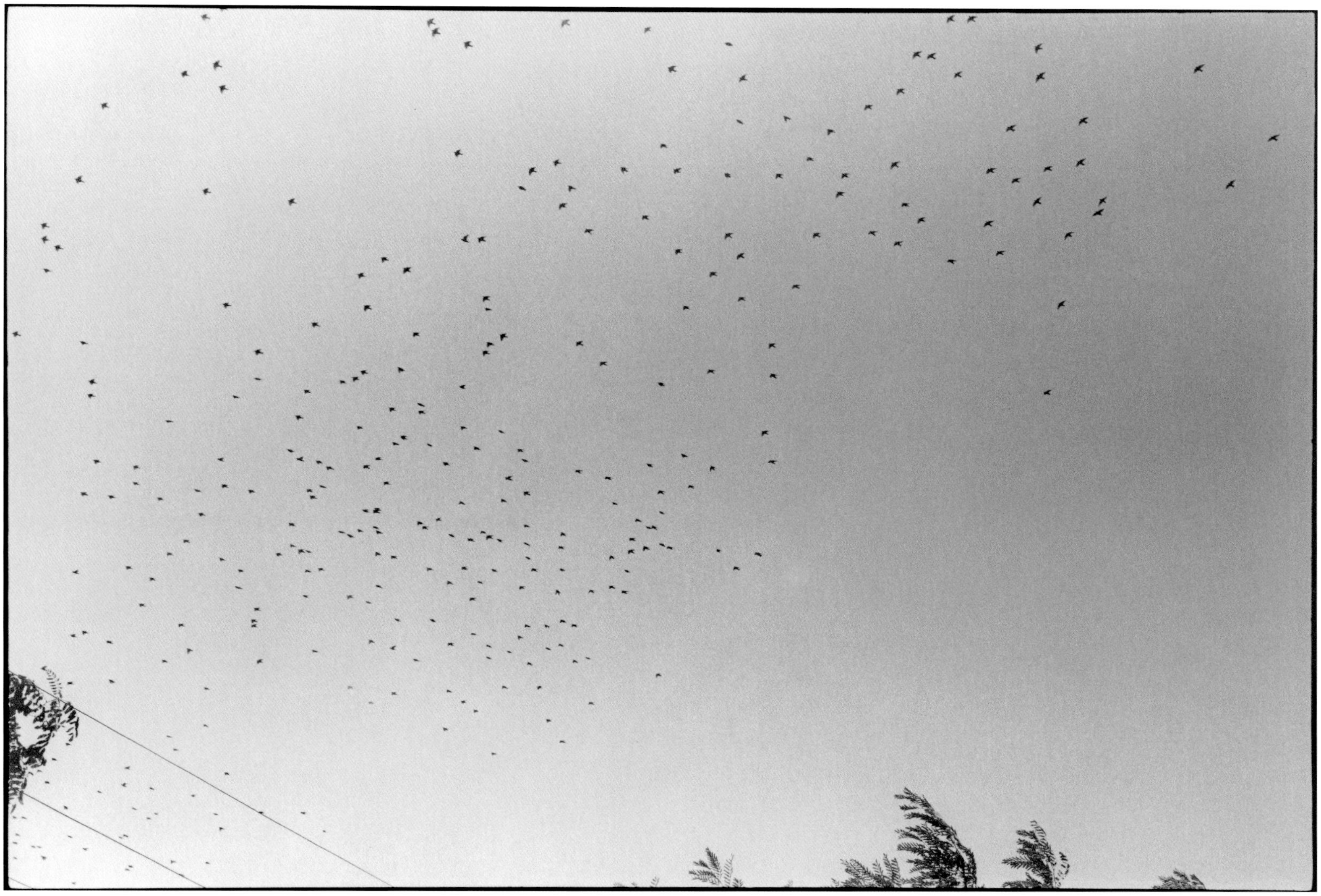

Legale Grenzflieger

Deutsch Jahrndorf, 1981

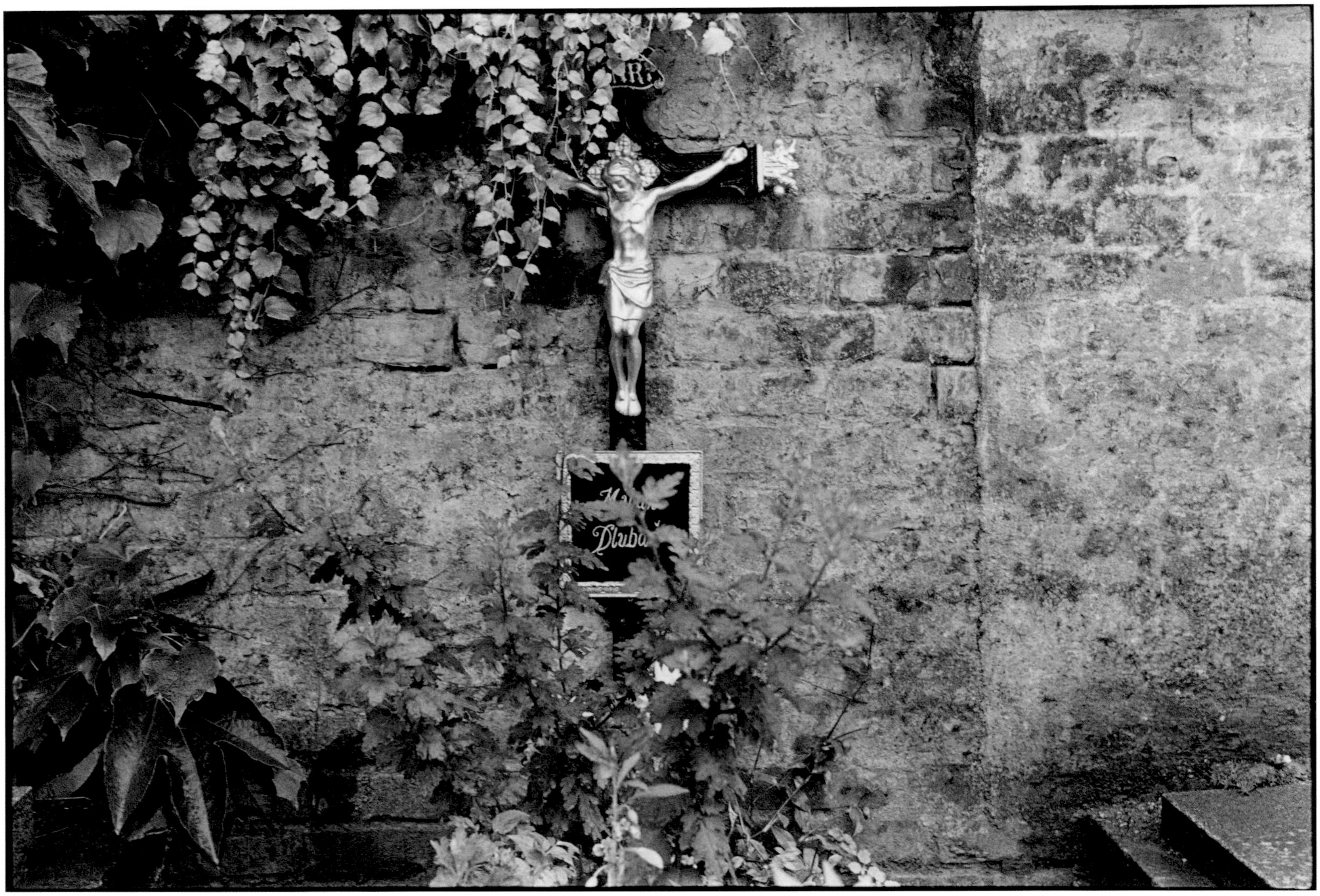

1980 hat Dlubač Milan, ein zweiundzwanzigjähriger Tscheche die hochwasserführende March schwimmend zu überqueren versucht, und es ist ihm auf Kosten seines Lebens gelungen.

Marchegg, 1981

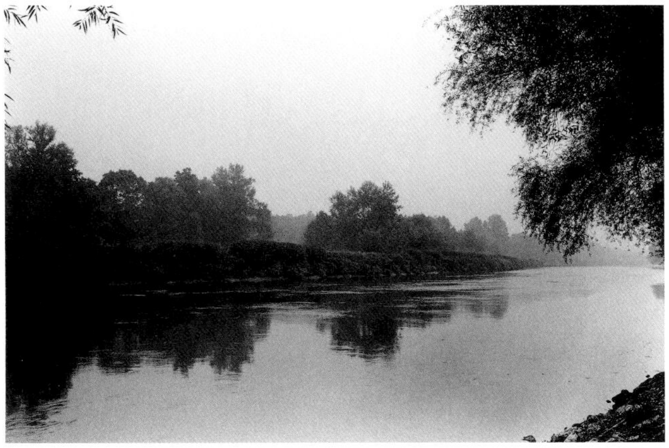

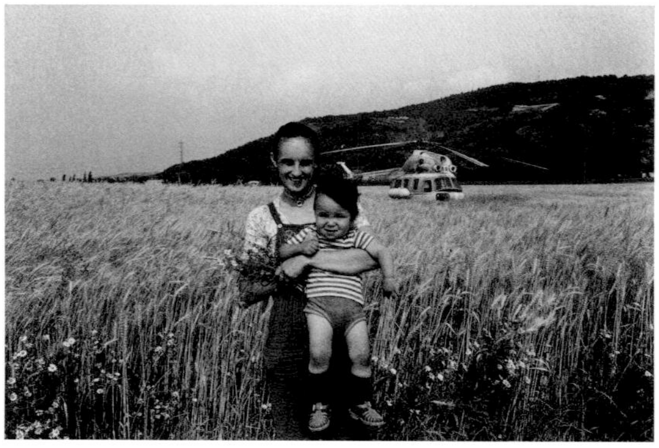

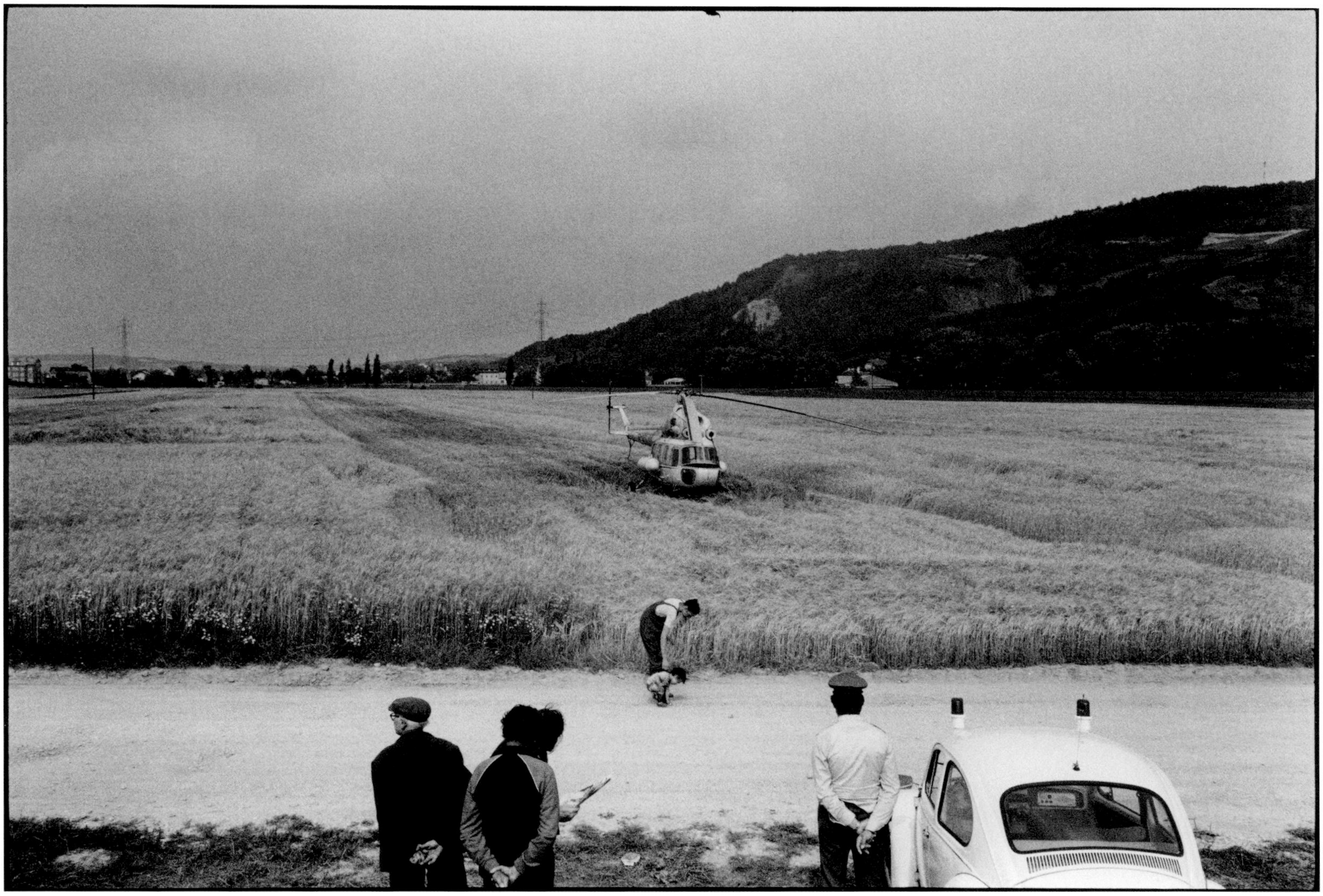

Polnische Flüchtlinge, ein Agrarpilot mit seiner Frau und seiner Tochter, landeten am 4. Juli 1982 mit einem Hubschrauber bei Wien. Ein Unwetter und eine geringe Flughöhe beim Überqueren der ČSSR haben ihnen dieses Abenteuer ermöglicht.

Langenzersdorf, 1982

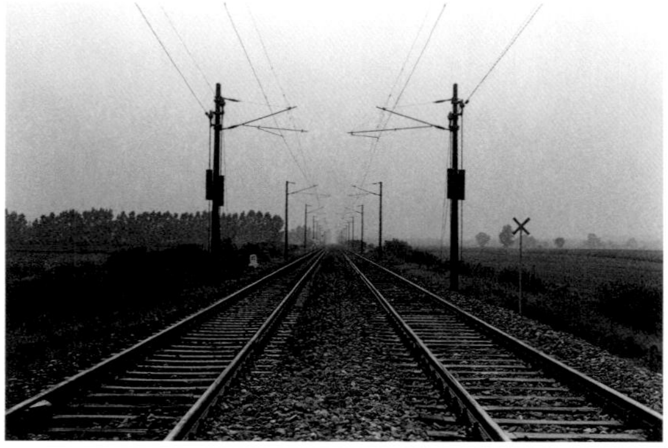

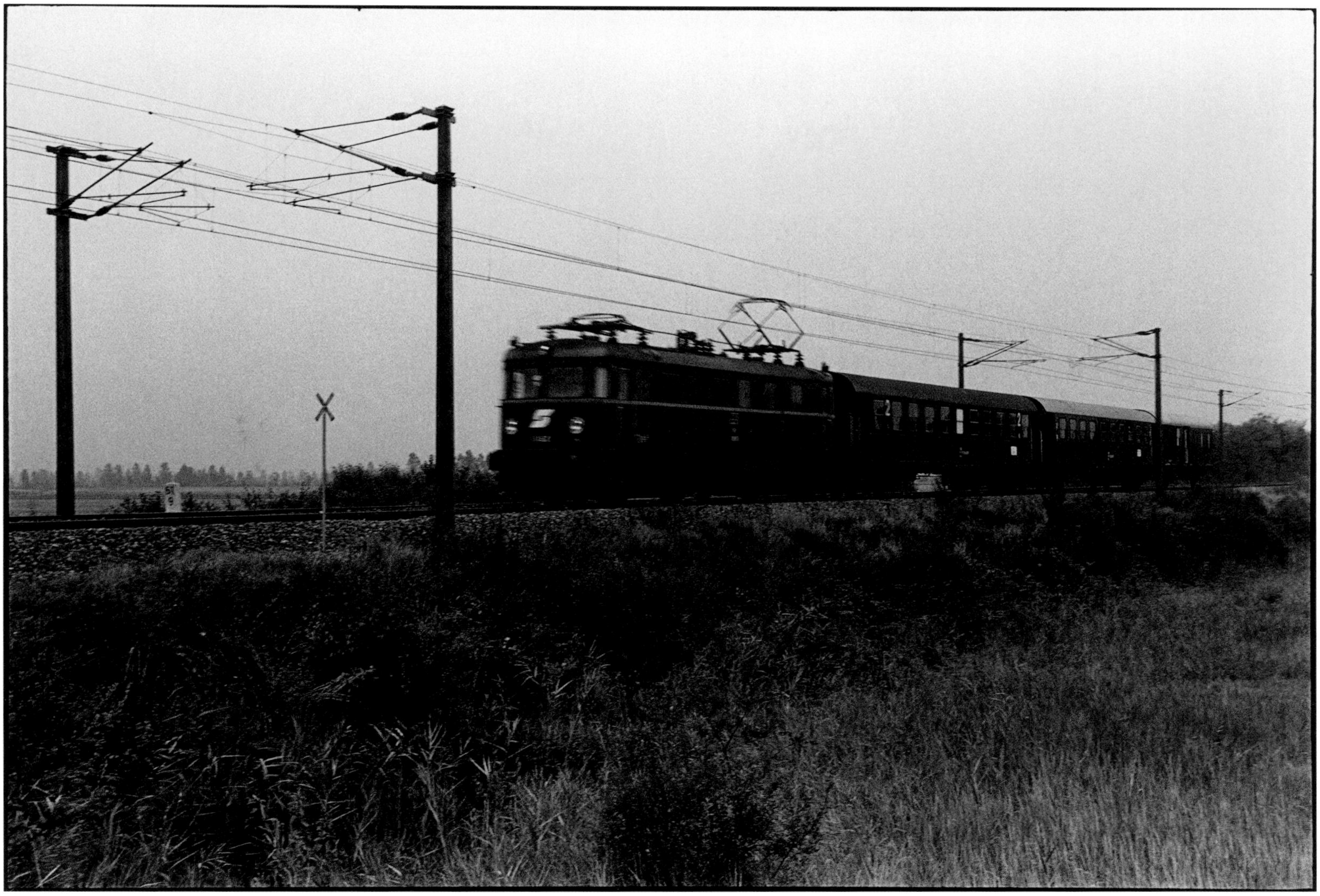

»In den letzten Jahren sind auf diesen Schienen der Bahnlinie Břeclav – Wien in den Güterzügen elf Flüchtlinge aus dem Osten nach Österreich gekommen.«

Drösing, 1983

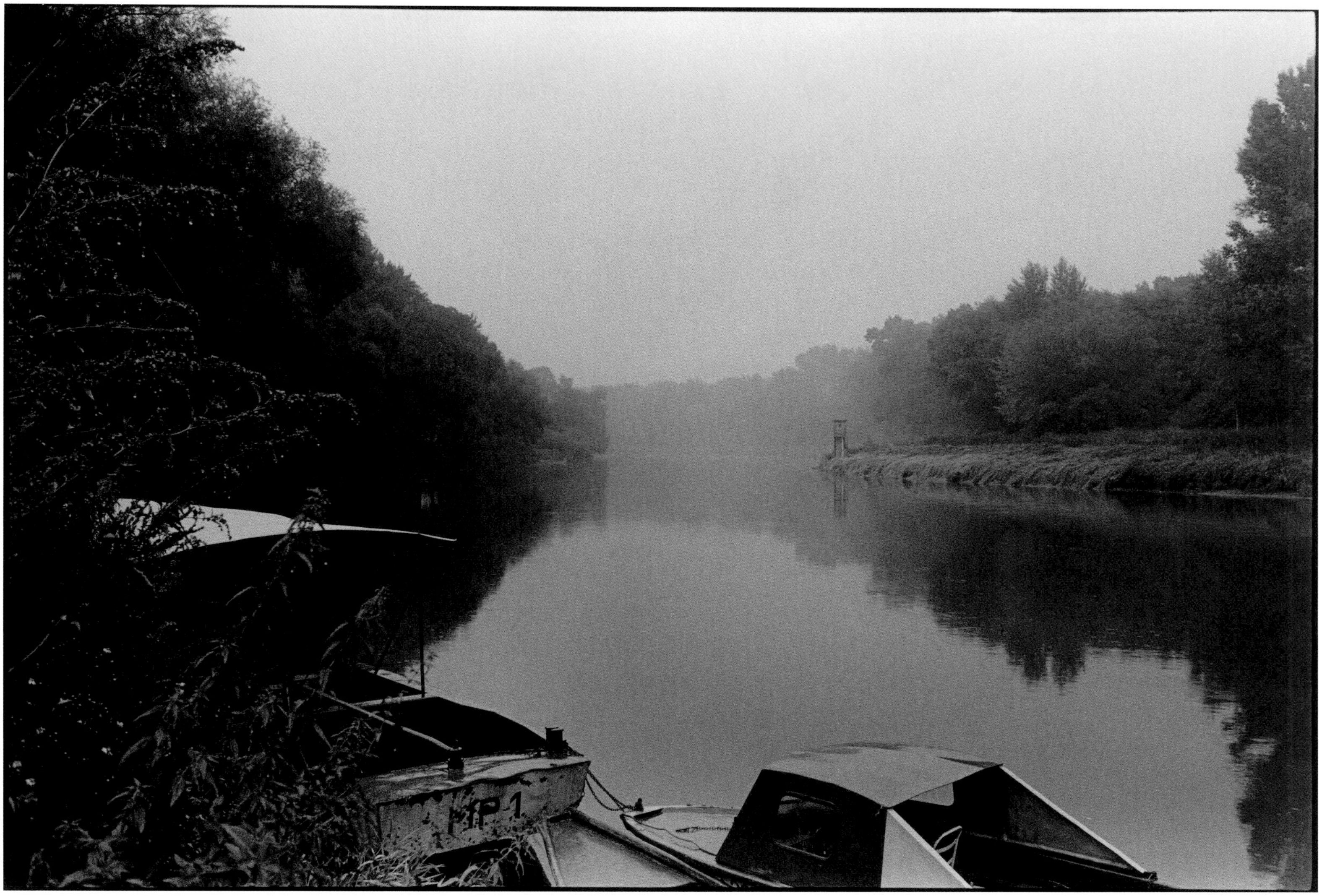

Grenzfluss March

Hohenau, 1981

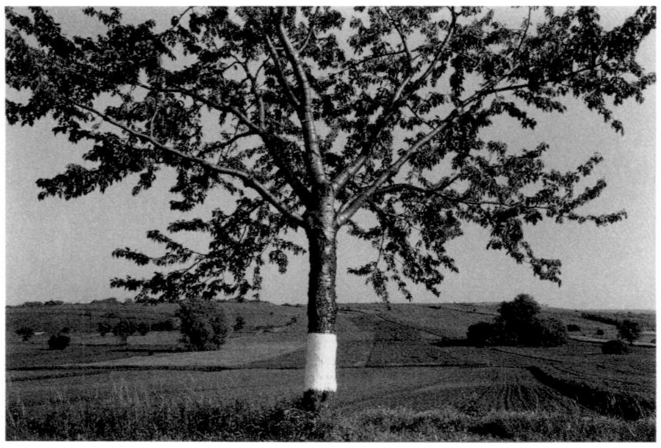

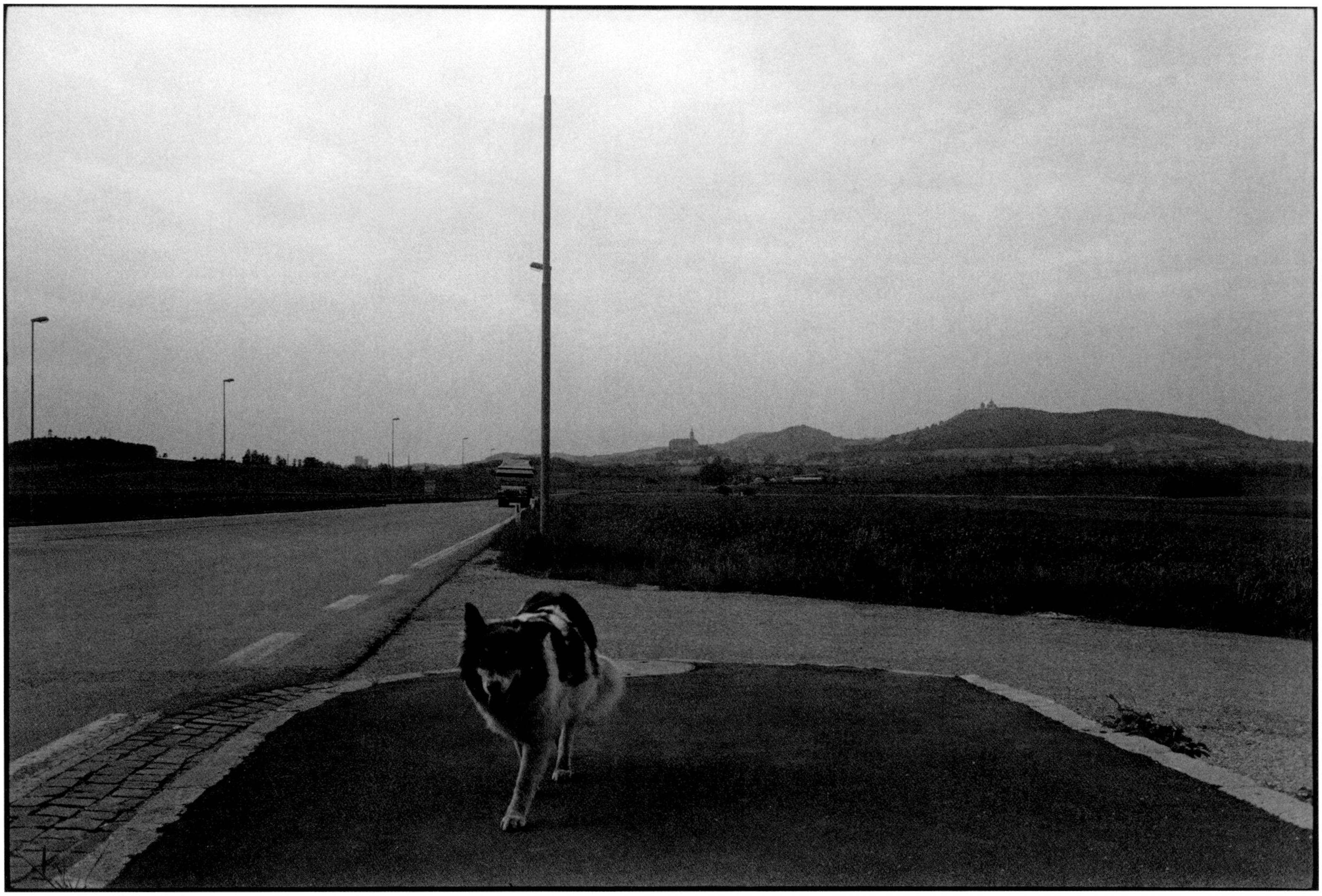

»Können Sie sich vorstellen, dass vor 1938 500 von 8000 Bewohnern Juden waren (Nikolsburg / Mikulov). Die Juden haben alles in der Hand gehabt. Gott sei Dank kam dann unser Führer und sie sind verschwunden! Dann haben wir aber die Stadt selbst verloren.«

Drasenhofen, 1983

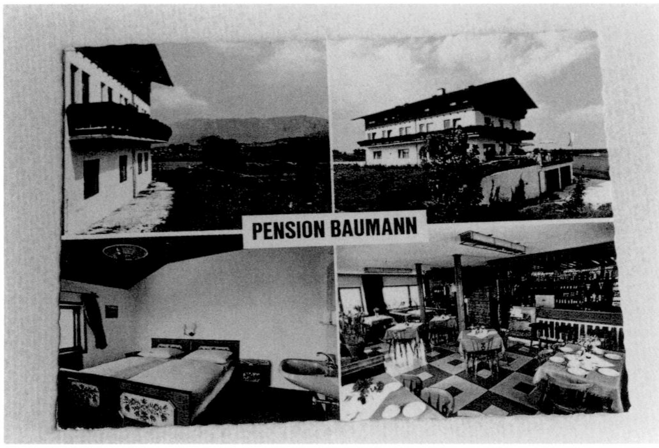
PENSION BAUMANN

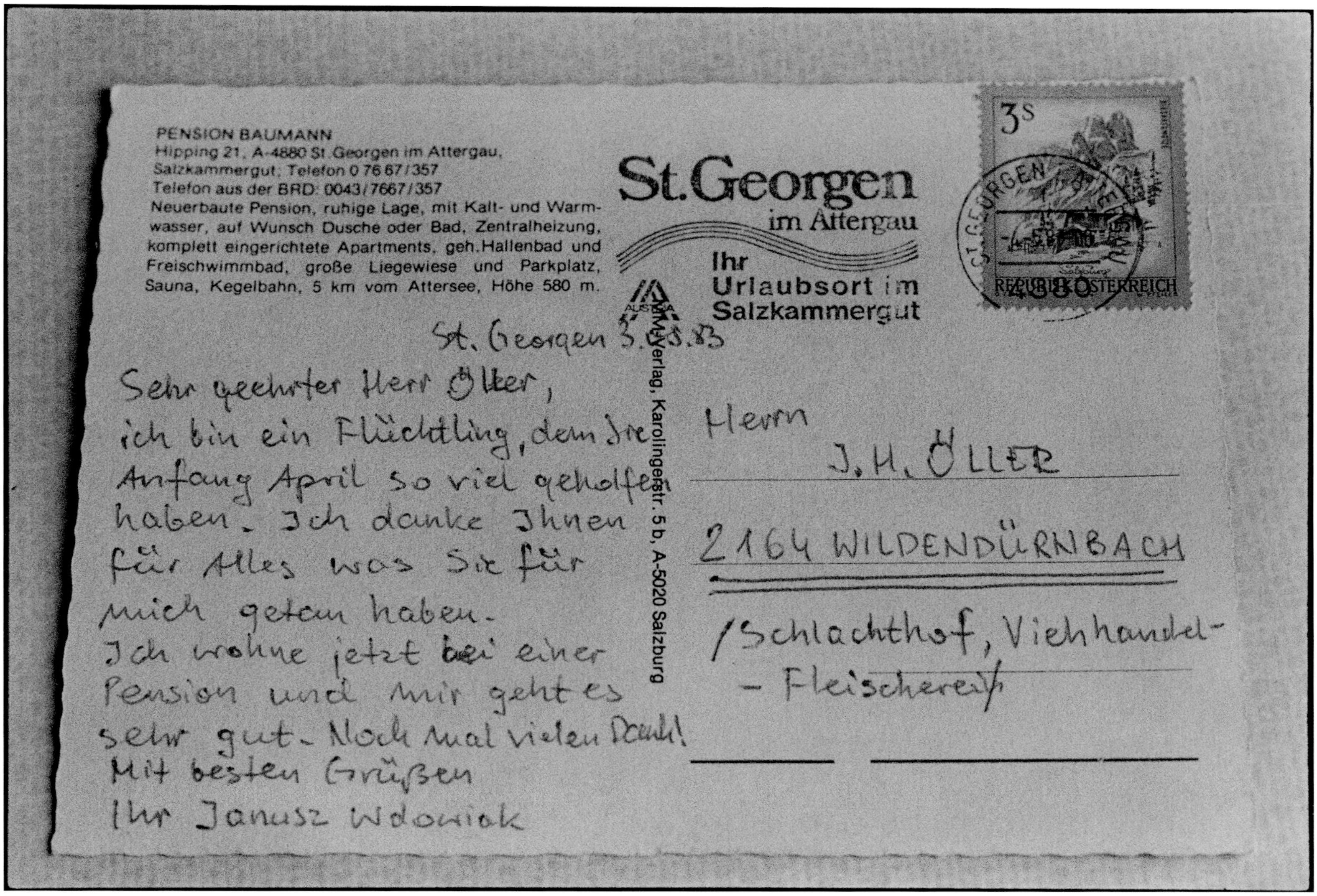

PENSION BAUMANN
Hipping 21, A-4880 St. Georgen im Attergau,
Salzkammergut; Telefon 0 76 67/357
Telefon aus der BRD: 0043/7667/357
Neuerbaute Pension, ruhige Lage, mit Kalt- und Warmwasser, auf Wunsch Dusche oder Bad, Zentralheizung, komplett eingerichtete Apartments, geh. Hallenbad und Freischwimmbad, große Liegewiese und Parkplatz, Sauna, Kegelbahn, 5 km vom Attersee, Höhe 580 m.

St. Georgen
im Attergau
Ihr Urlaubsort im Salzkammergut

Verlag, Karolingerstr. 5 b, A-5020 Salzburg

3 S
REPUBLIK ÖSTERREICH

St. Georgen 3.05.83

Sehr geehrter Herr Öller,
ich bin ein Flüchtling, dem Sie Anfang April so viel geholfen haben. Ich danke Ihnen für Alles was Sie für mich getan haben.
Ich wohne jetzt bei einer Pension und mir geht es sehr gut. Noch mal vielen Dank!
Mit besten Grüßen
Ihr Janusz Wdowiak

Herrn
J. H. ÖLLER
2164 WILDENDÜRNBACH
/Schlachthof, Viehhandel-
– Fleischerei/

»Vor vier Wochen um 21.00 Uhr ist ein Pole nur in Unterhosen und mit seinen Reisedokumenten, ganz nass vor unserer Türe gestanden. Er hat gesagt, er ist über die Thaya geschwommen und dann dem Gaslicht bei unserer Erdgasquelle nachgegangen. Schon vorher haben wir es dauernd Schießen gehört. Bis nach Mitternacht war die Grenze hell beleuchtet. Er hat bei uns geduscht und gegessen. Wir haben ihm Kleider gegeben und die Gendarmerie aus Laa an der Thaya geholt.«

Wildendürnbach, 1983

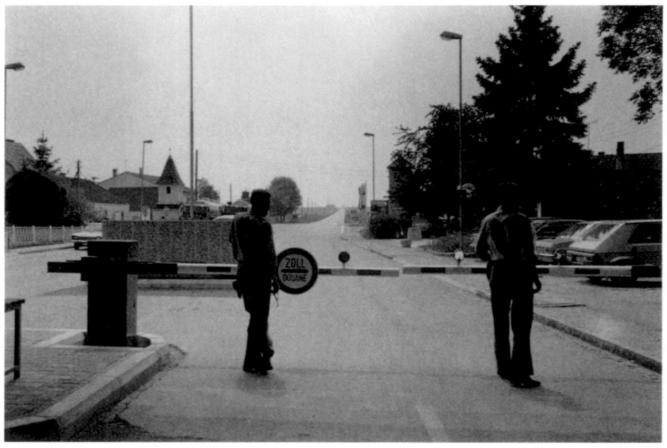
ZOLL
DOUANE

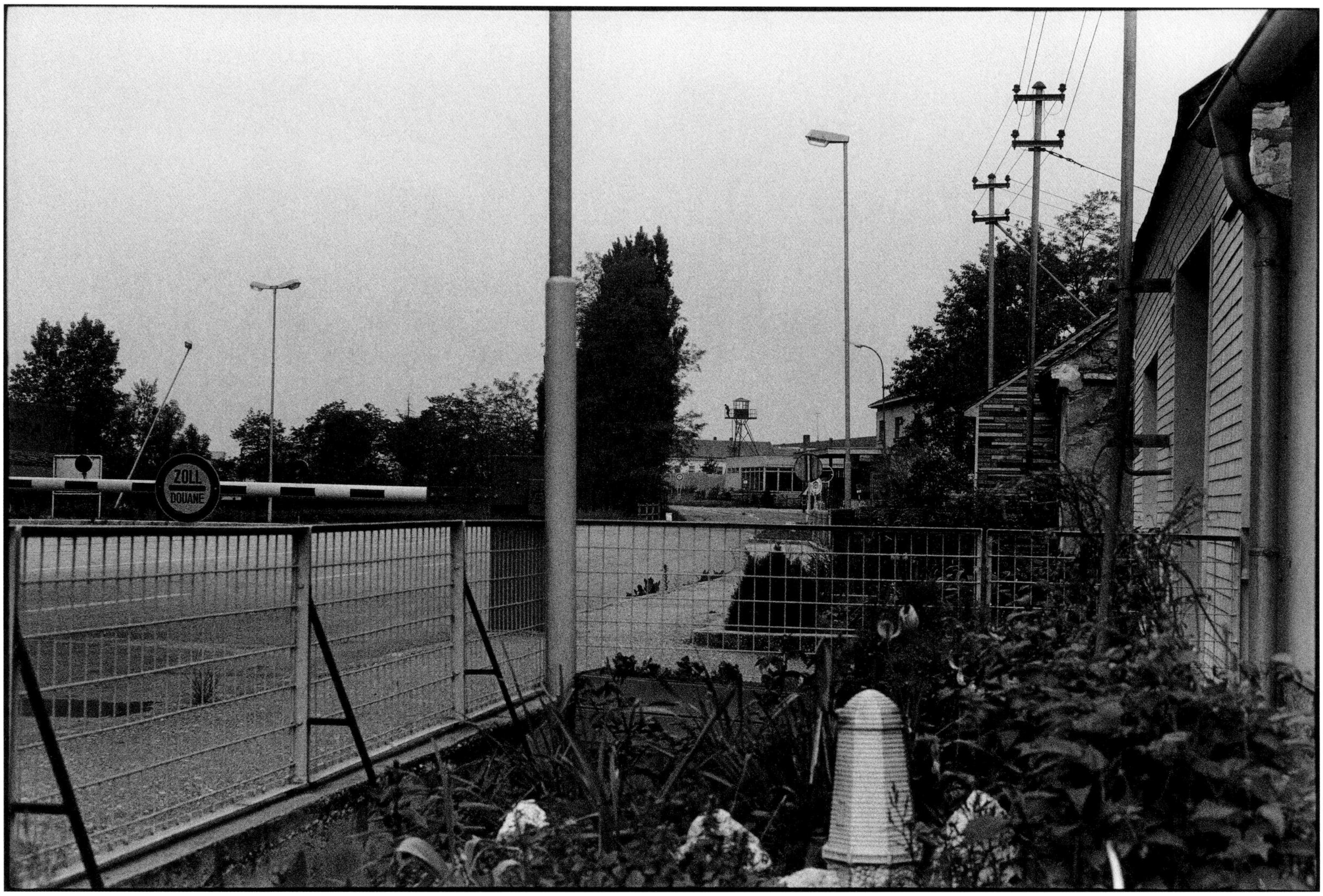

Grenzübergang

Kleinhaugsdorf, 1983

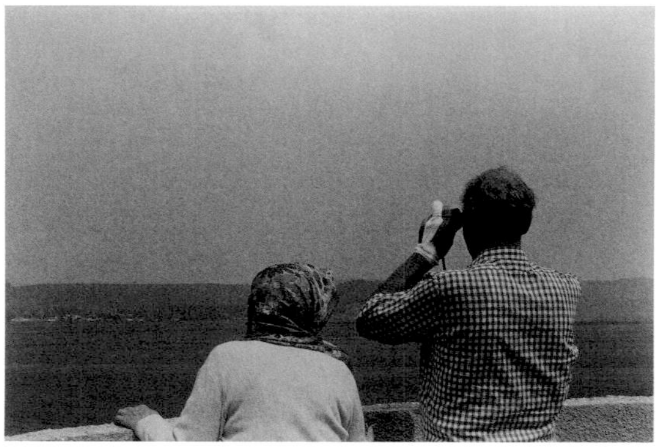

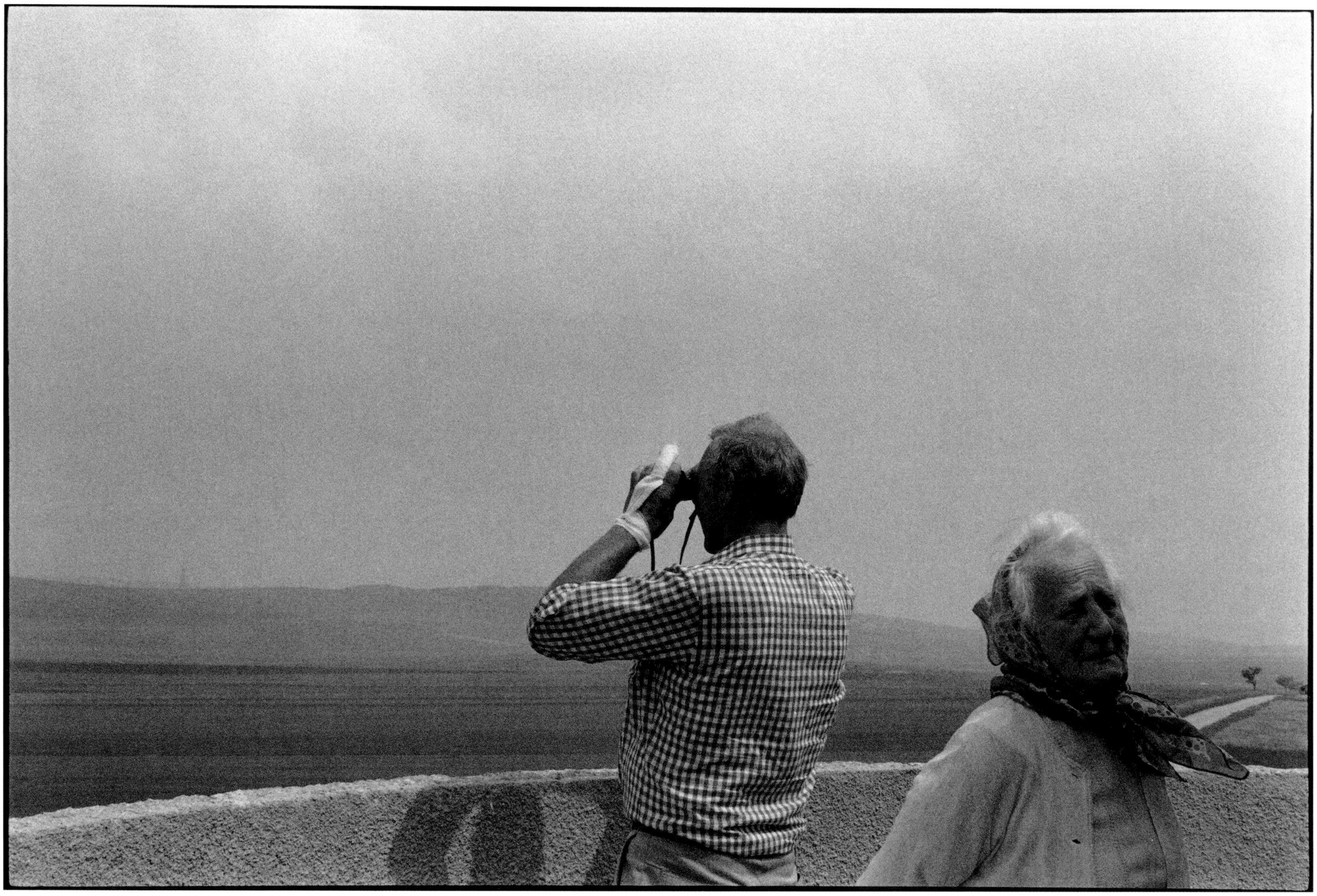

»Ich bin Zigeunerin. Unsere Heimat liegt dort drüben. Achtunddreißig Jahre ist es jetzt her, ja 1945, sind wir nur mit den Kleidern am Leib und ein paar Binkel ausgetrieben worden. In Österreich konnten wir nicht bleiben, da sind wir nach Deutschland gegangen. Ich habe meine Heimat nie vergessen und auch nicht, wie wir von dort weggegangen sind.«

Unterretzbach, 1983

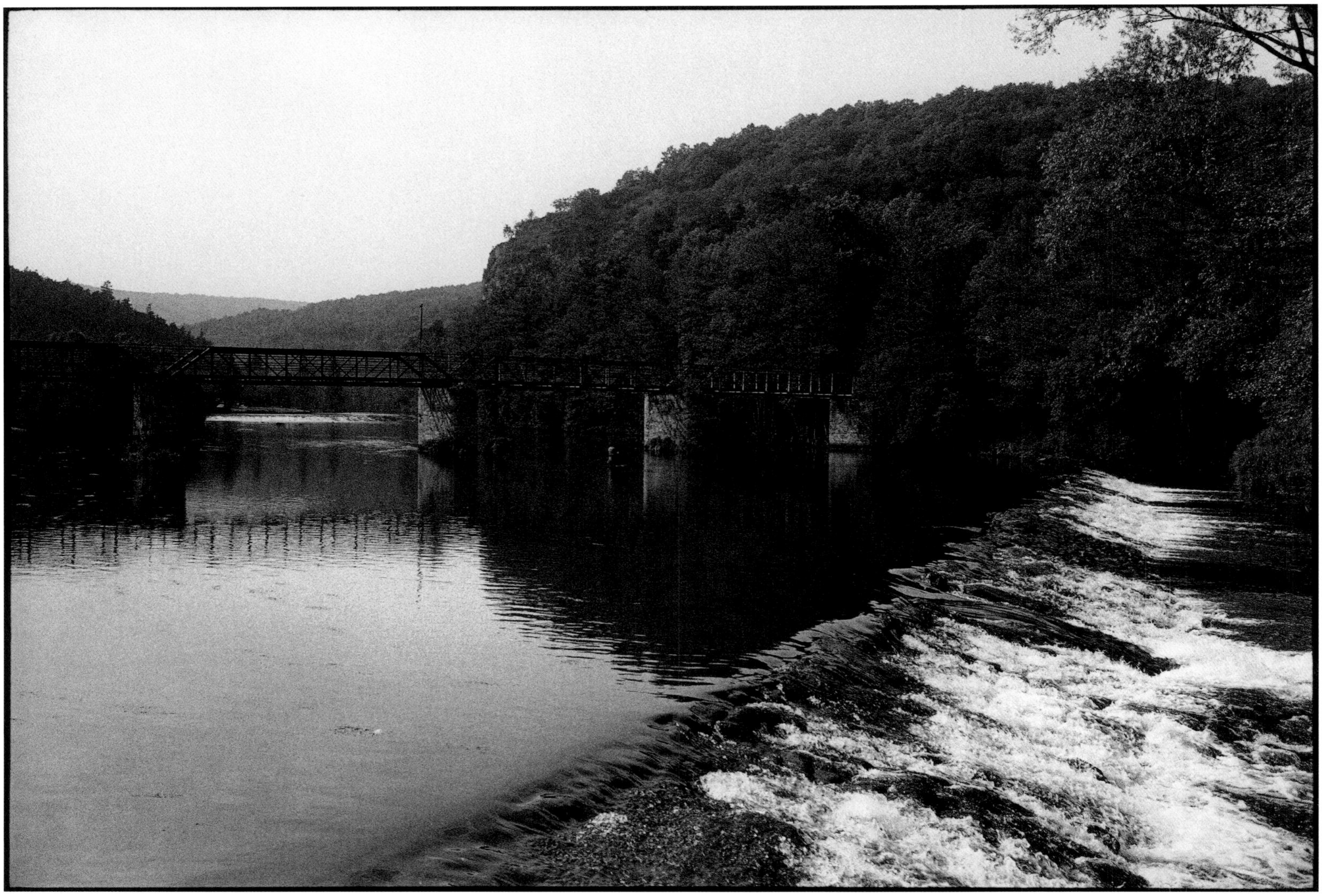

»Ich war noch ein kleiner Bub, wie damals Hitler in einem Cabriolet aus Znaim über diese Brücke gefahren ist. Am Berg gegenüber haben sie damals eine riesige Hakenkreuzfahne aufgehängt und wir Kinder haben ihn mit unseren Hakenkreuzflaggen begrüßt. 1968, während der Dubček-Zeit, sollte die Brücke wieder als Grenzübergang geöffnet werden. Die Österreicher haben damals die halbe Brücke grün, die Tschechen ihre Hälfte grau gestrichen, Aber ein Jahr später, nachdem Dubček gestürzt worden war, sind Panzer gekommen und haben die Fahrbahn abgetragen. Seither ist es wieder ganz ruhig da.«

Hardegg, 1983

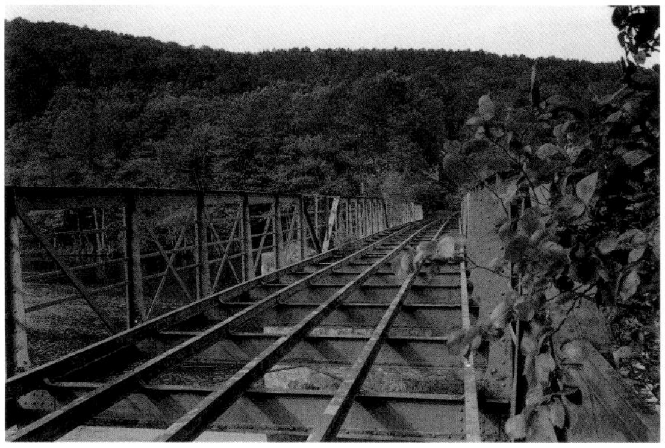

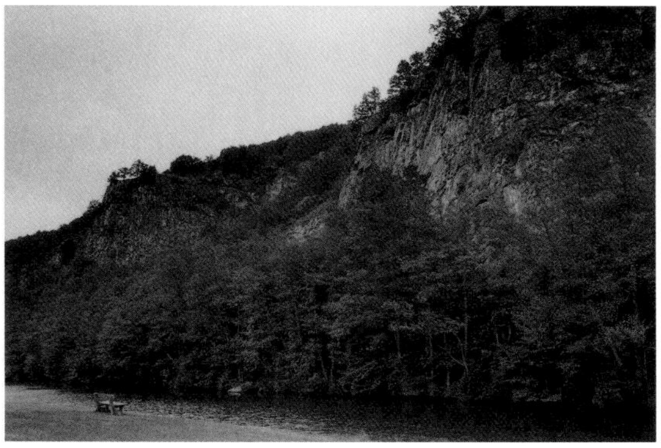

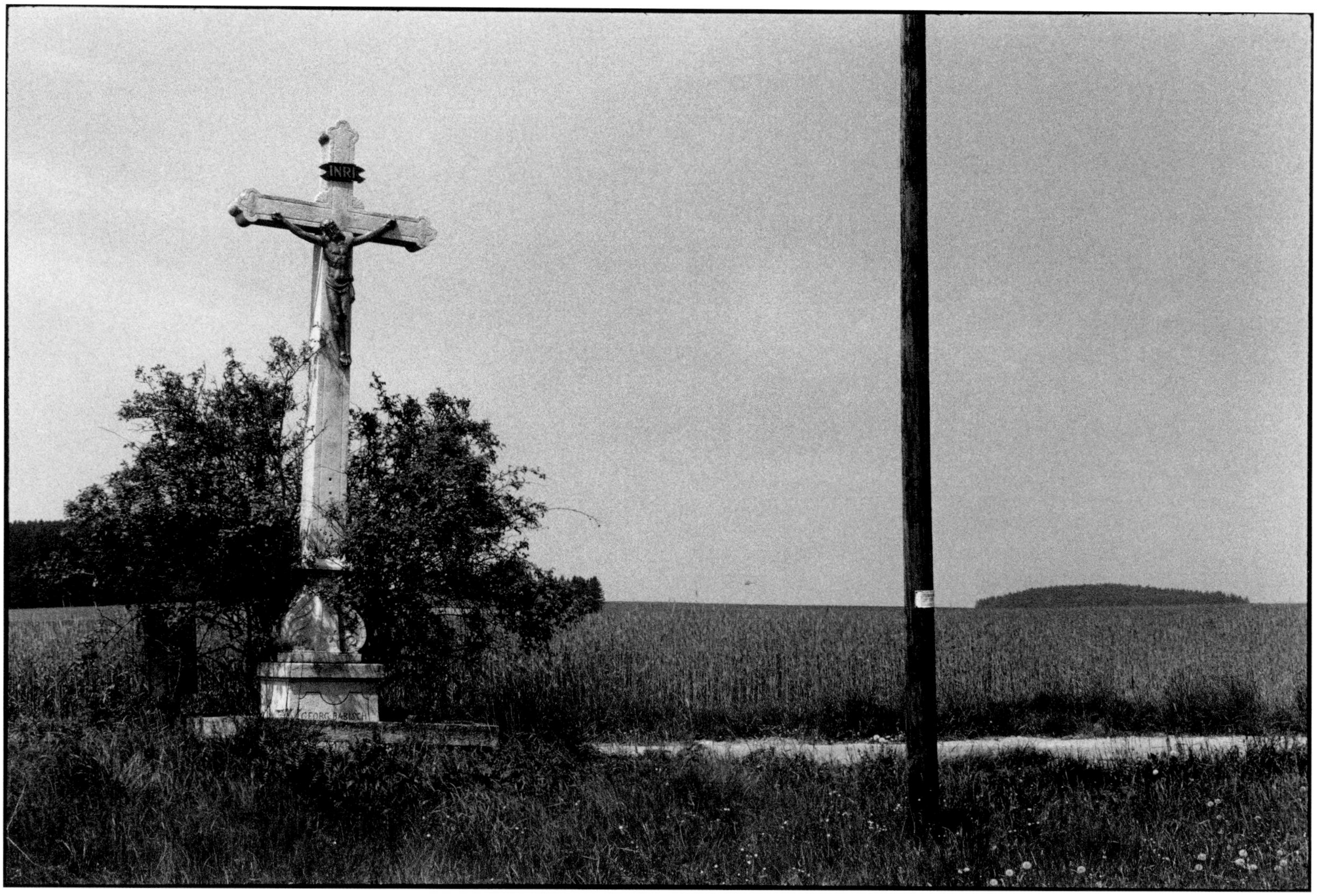

Ein tschechischer Militärhubschrauber, der entlang der Grenze seinen Kontrollflug macht.

Fratres, 1983

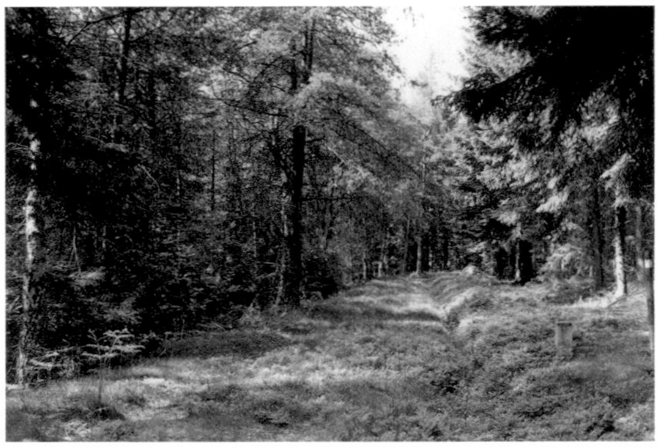

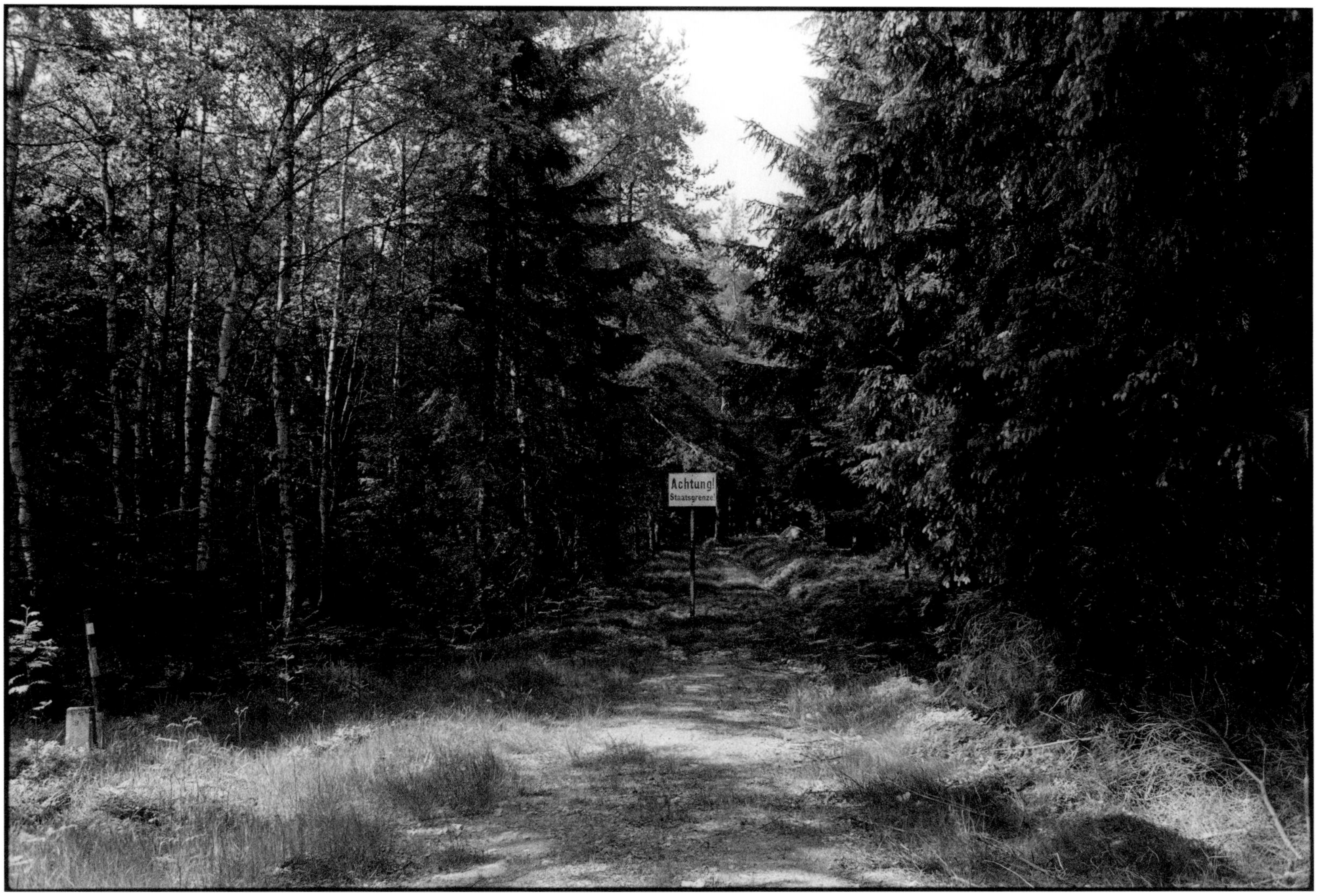

»Voriges Jahr im Spätsommer ist ein Gendarm von hier beim Schwammerlsuchen über die Grenze auf tschechisches Gebiet gekommen. Er ist verhaftet worden. Je nach Alter, Geschlecht und Beruf muss man mit einem längeren oder kürzeren Aufenthalt rechnen. Er ist nach zwei Tagen überstellt worden.«

Kautzen, 1983

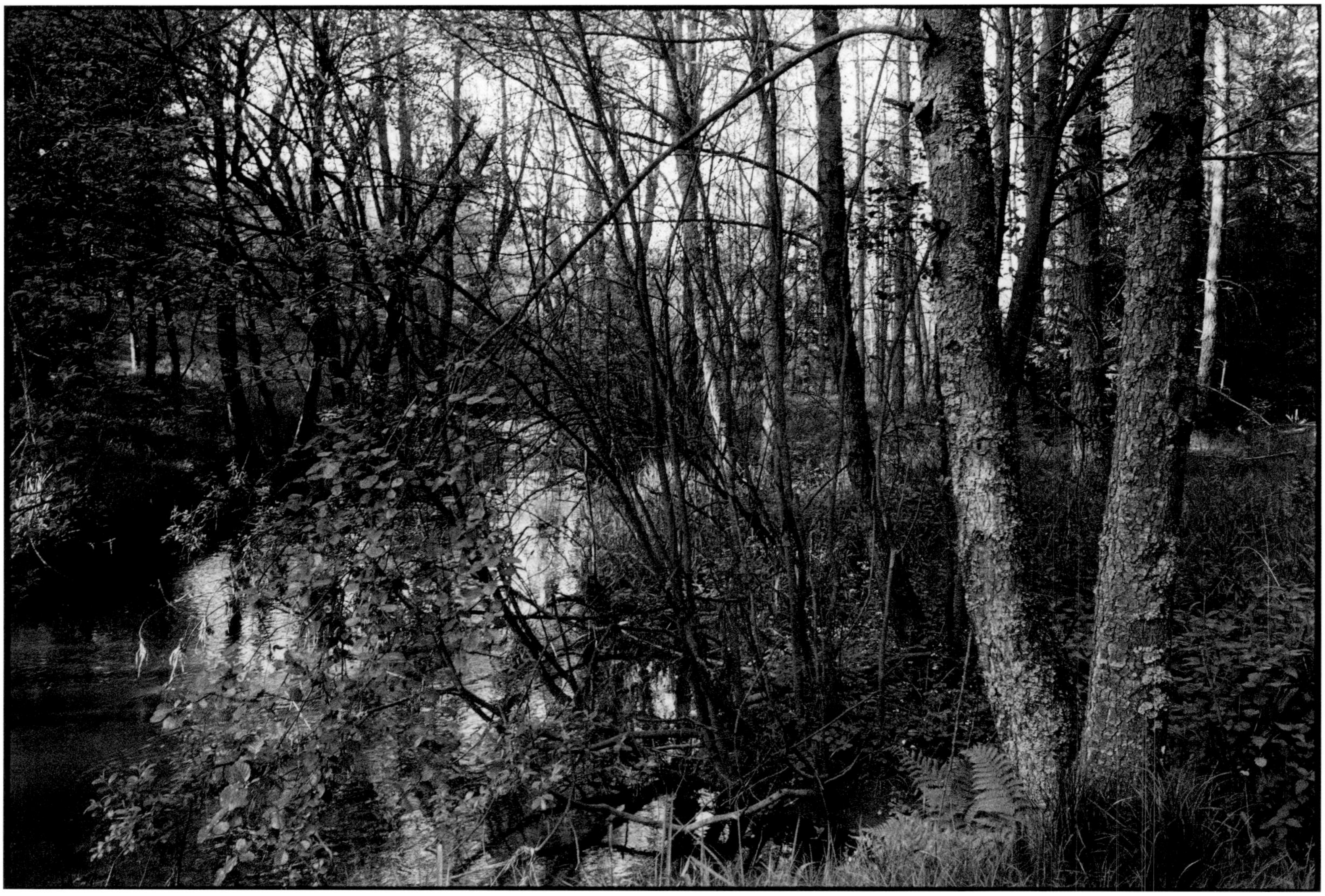

Der nördlichste Punkt Österreichs

Rottal, 1983

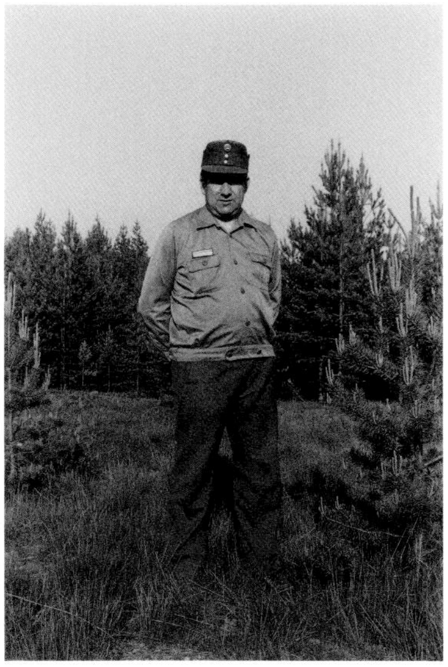

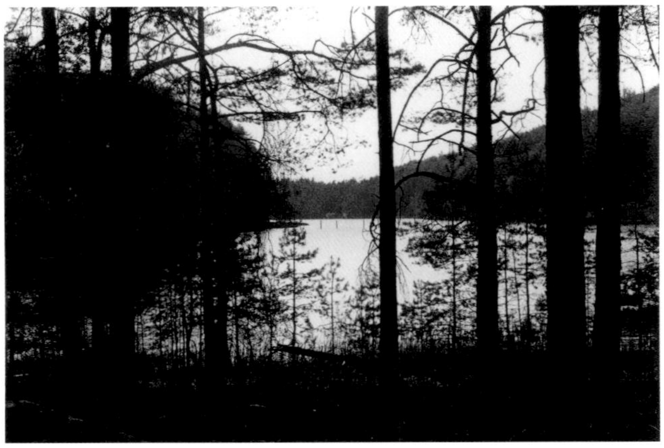

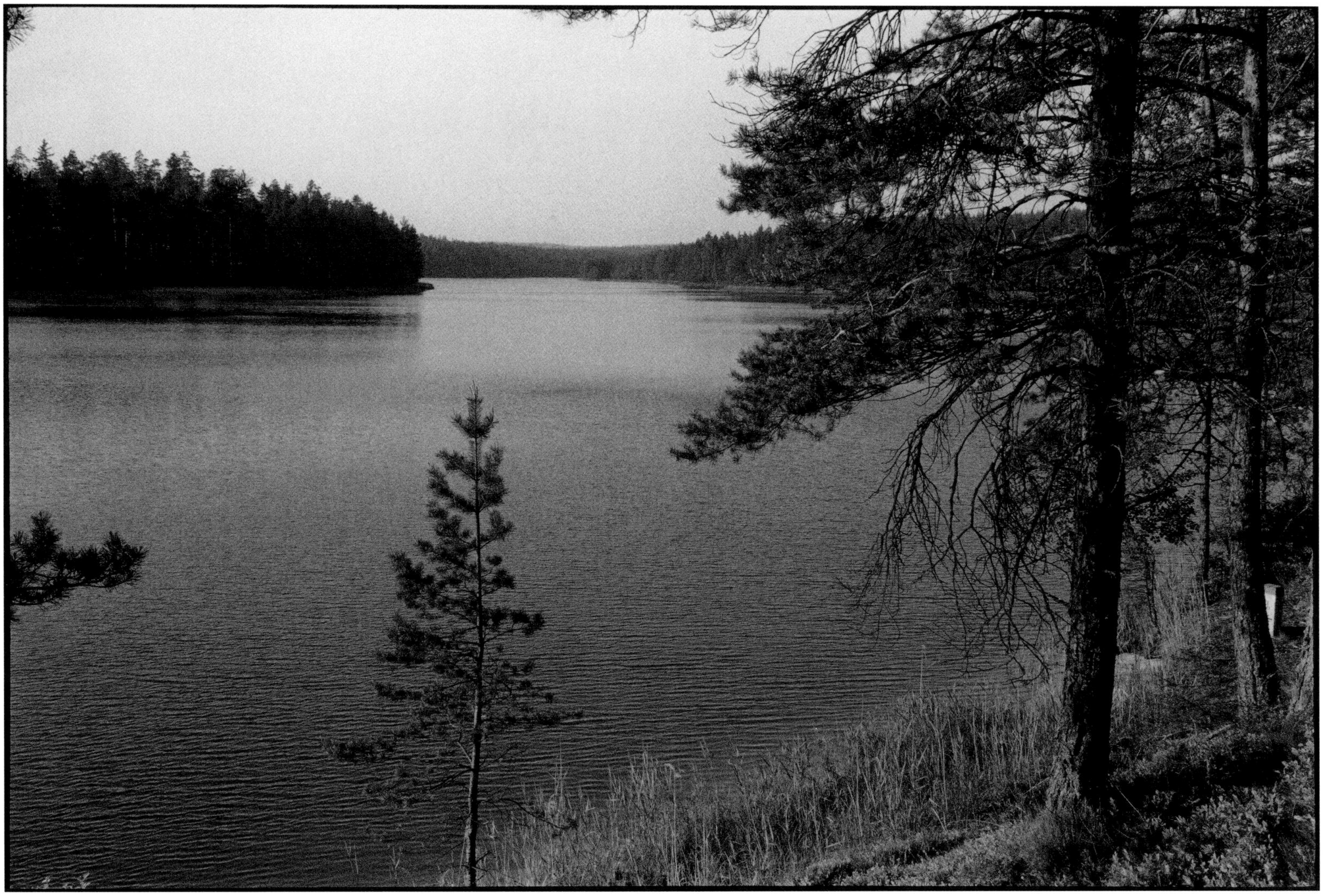

»Vor vier Jahren flüchtete ein Tscheche mit dem Taucheranzug durch den Teich nach Österreich. Nach diesem Vorfall hat Tschechien im Teich ein durchgehendes Netz gespannt.«

Stankauer Teich / Staňkovský rybník, 1983

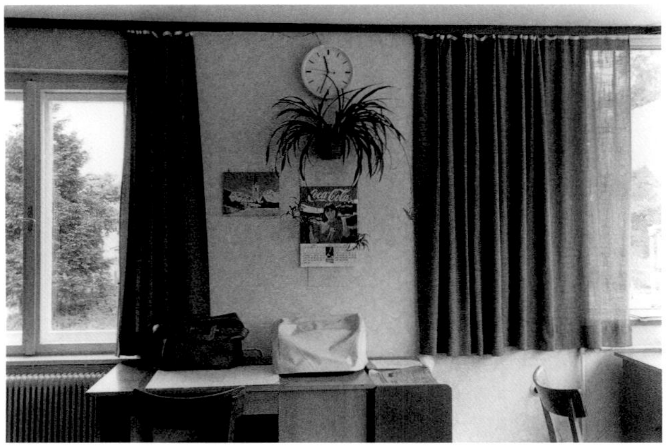
Coca-Cola

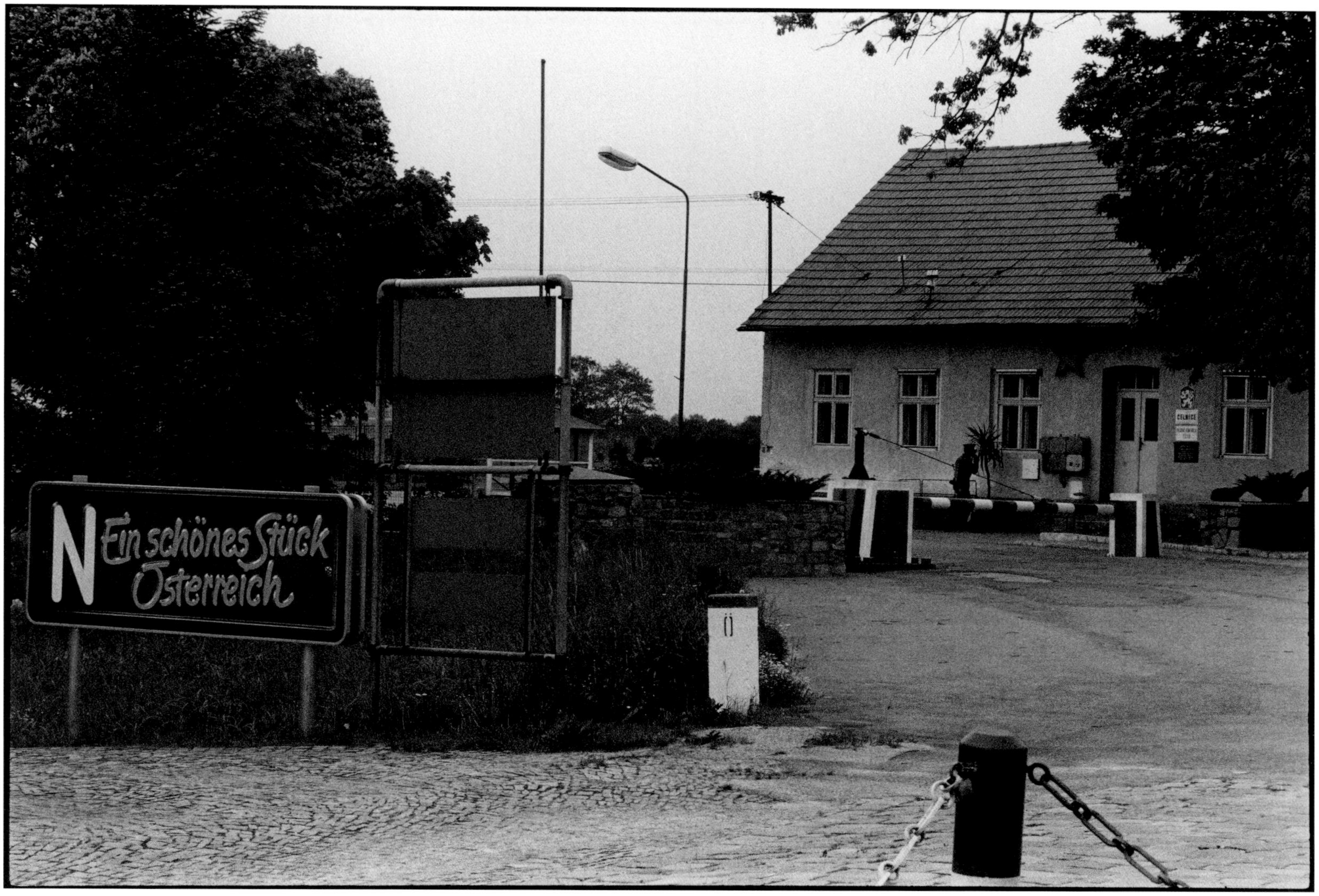

»Hier ist Berlin in Österreich. Durch die Stadt geht ein dreifacher Grenzzaun und die Leute drüben leben unter einem anderen politischen Regime. Ich bin ehrlich gesagt lieber auf dieser Seite.«

Gmünd, 1983

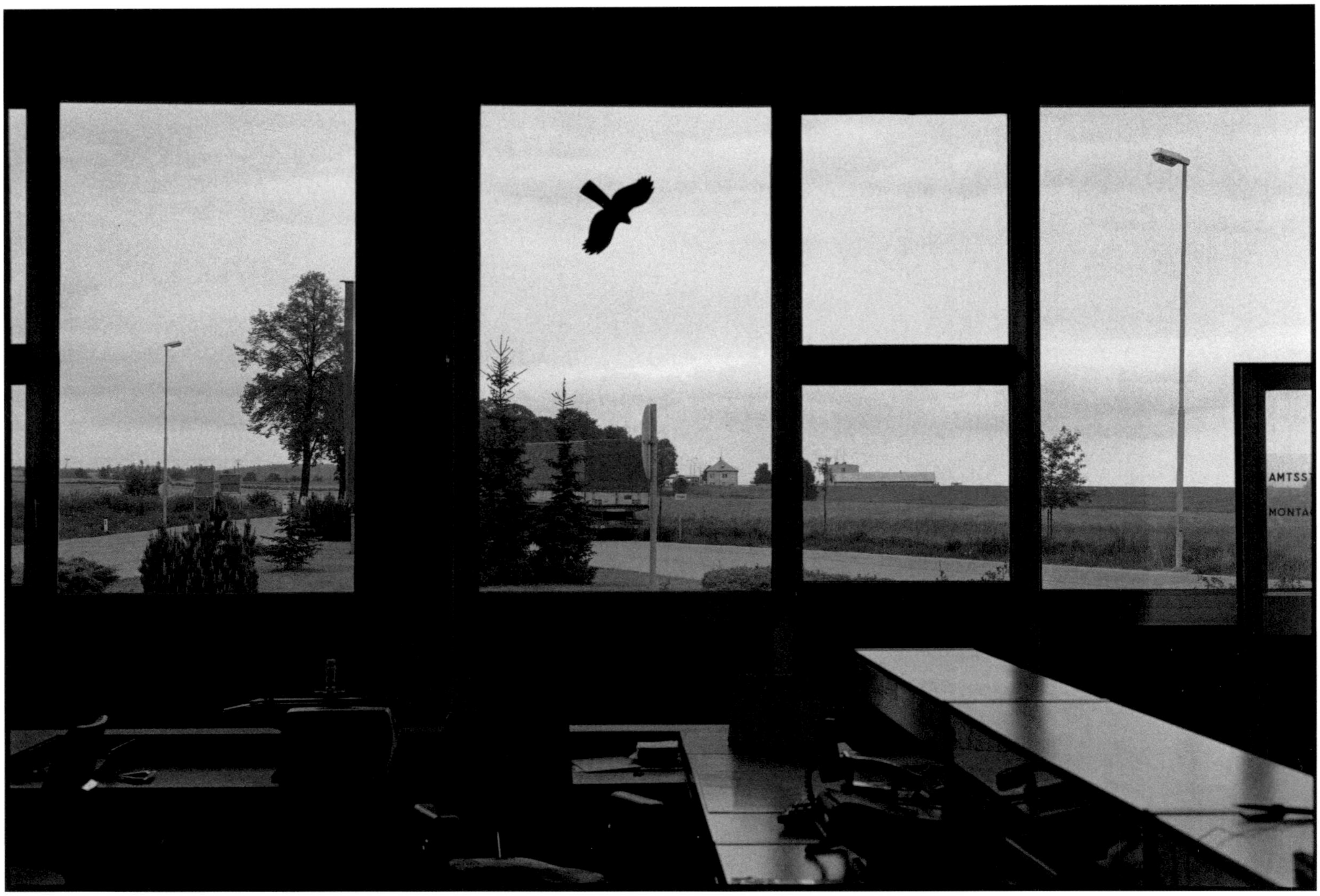

»Vor vier Jahren ist hier das neue Zollhaus gebaut worden. Viele Vögel sind damals täglich gegen die Glasscheiben geflogen und gestorben. Wir haben uns beim Naturschutz erkundigt und ein Pickerl, ich glaube aus der Schweiz bekommen. Seither ist Ruhe.«

Weigetschlag, 1983

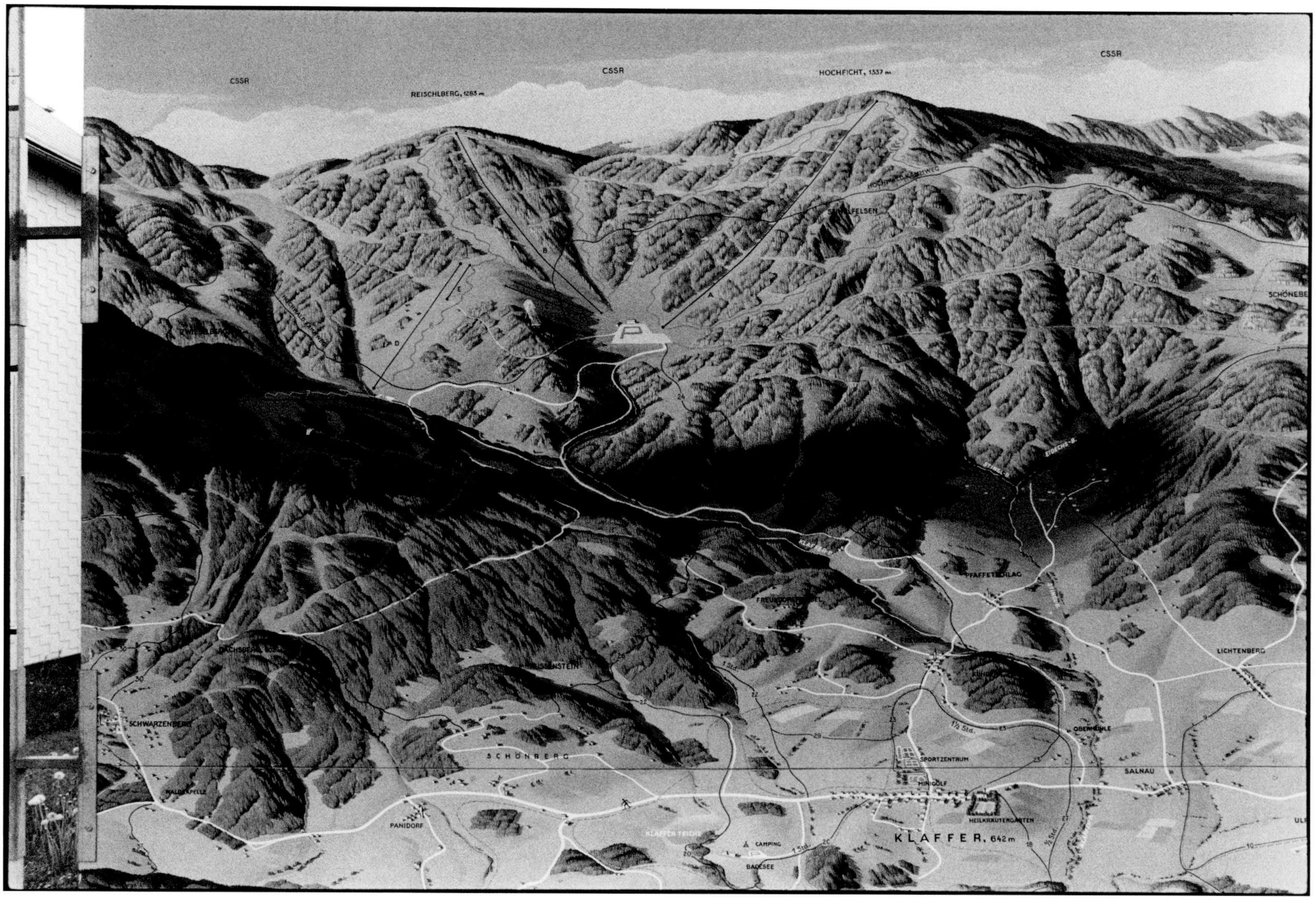

Grenzgebirge Böhmerwald

Klaffer am Hochficht, 1983

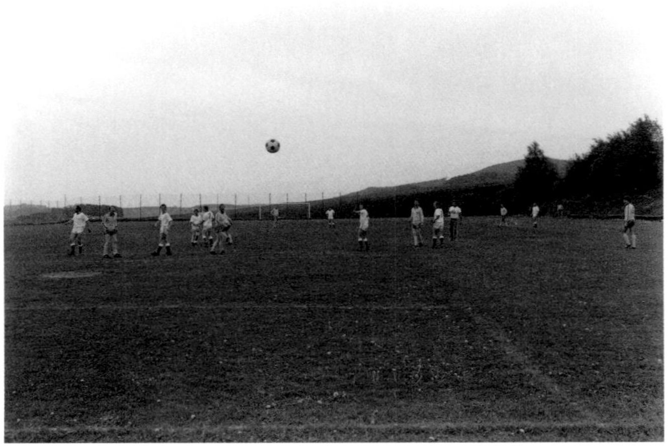

1 Wurzenpass
2 Loiblpass
3 Seebergsattel
4 Globasnitz / Globasnica
5 Südsteirische Weinstraße
6 Spielfeld
7 Radkersburg
8 Rattersdorf
9 Loipersbach im Burgenland
10 Loipersbach im Burgenland
11 Schattendorf
12 Andau
13 Deutsch Jahrndorf
14 Marchegg
15 Langenzersdorf
16 Drösing
17 Hohenau
18 Drasenhofen
19 Wildendürnbach
20 Kleinhaugsdorf
21 Unterretzbach
22 Hardegg
23 Fratres
24 Kauzen
25 Rottal
26 Stankauer Teich / Staňkovský rybník
27 Gmünd
28 Weigetschlag
29 Klaffer am Hochficht

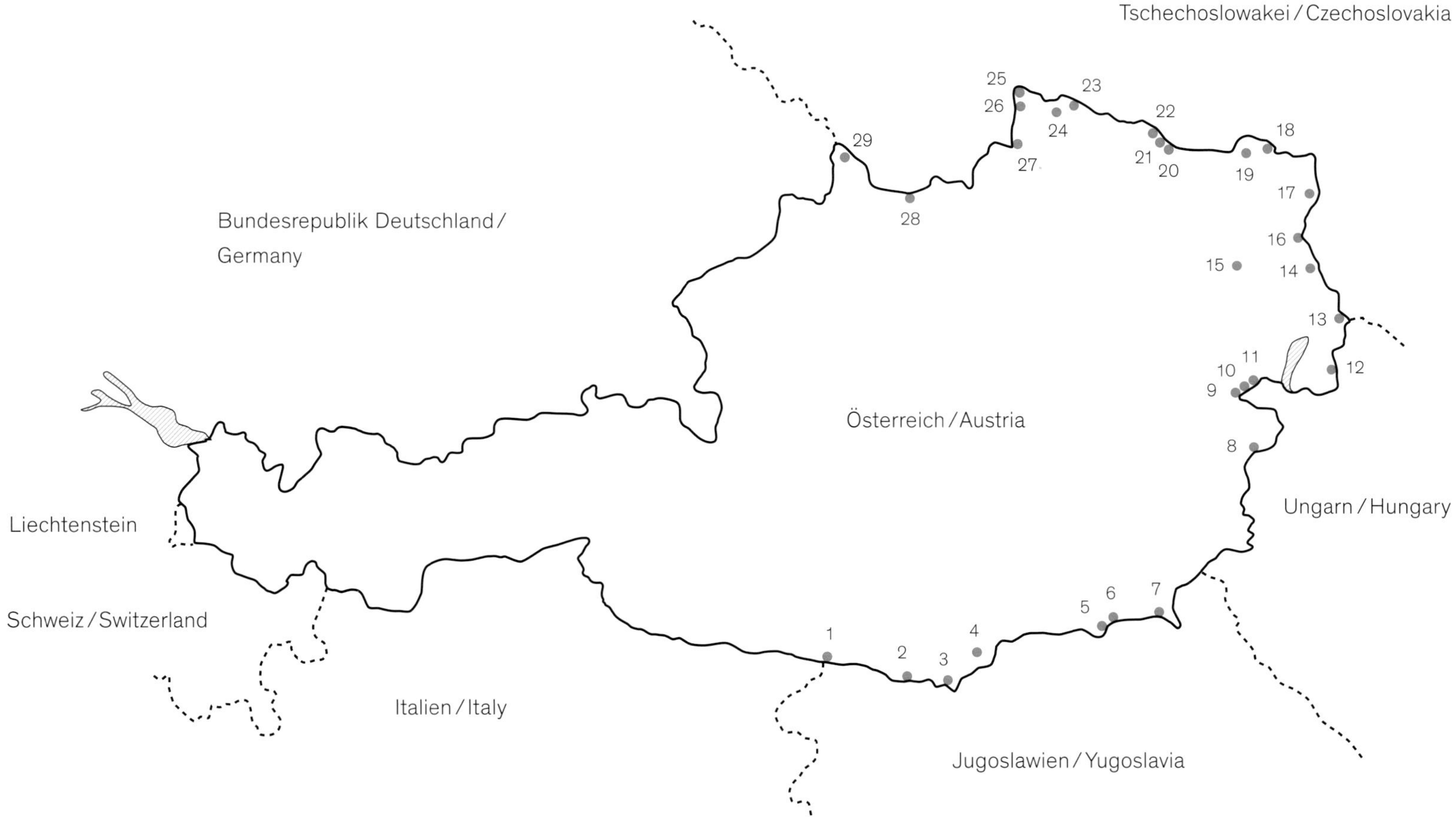

Tschechoslowakei / Czechoslovakia
Bundesrepublik Deutschland / Germany
Österreich / Austria
Ungarn / Hungary
Liechtenstein
Schweiz / Switzerland
Italien / Italy
Jugoslawien / Yugoslavia
1
2
3
4
5
6
7
8
9
10
11
12
13
14
15
16
17
18
19
20
21
22
23
24
25
26
27
28
29

Staatsgrenze 1981 – 1983

Österreich grenzt an sieben Aus-Länder:
die Bundesrepublik Deutschland, die Tschechoslowakei, Ungarn, Jugoslawien, Italien, die Schweiz und Liechtenstein, Staaten der verschiedensten politischen Richtungen: sogenannte Ostblockstaaten, freie westliche Länder, einen neutralen Staat und ein Fürstentum.

Künstlich, politisch gezogene Grenzlinien haben immer wieder eine wichtige Rolle für die Menschen gespielt, und so wird es wohl bleiben, solange es Menschen gibt. Ich glaube, solche Linien werden erst dann aufhören wichtig zu sein, wenn es gilt, sich gemeinsam gegen einen Außerirdischen abzugrenzen.

Die 2706 km lange österreichische Grenze ist weit weniger brutal als z. B. die Grenze in Berlin, wo eine Betonmauer grausam eine Stadt halbiert. Sie ist sogar schön, romantisch, unauffällig. Aber gerade in dieser ruhigen Landschaft spürt man die stillen, traurigen Tatsachen umso stärker.

Ich habe auf meiner Reise durch das Grenzgebiet versucht, Orte und Plätze aufzusuchen, an denen sich tragische Zwischenfälle ereigneten, und mich nach kleinen persönlichen Geschichten umzuhören, um mich mit ihrer Hilfe an das Thema »Grenze« heranzutasten.

Seiichi Furuya, 1983

Vor sieben Jahren habe ich die Arbeit »Staatsgrenze Teil I« (Grenze zu den Ostblock-Staaten) beendet. Ende der achtziger Jahre ist ein aus Moskau kommender »revolutionärer« Taifun von Norden nach Süden über Mitteleuropa hinweggezogen. Es sieht heute so aus, als wäre das Auge des Taifuns über dem Balkan stehen geblieben.

Was die österreichische Grenze zum »Ostblock« angeht, wurde dieses nach dem Zweiten Weltkrieg geschaffene Symbol politischer und menschlicher Schicksale weggerissen. Die Grenze als Schicksal gehört der Vergangenheit an — zumindest die sichtbaren Sperren sind verschwunden.

Eine Arbeit wie »Staatsgrenze« wäre heute nicht mehr möglich — sie ist selbst bereits Geschichte geworden, was mich freut. Man darf dabei aber nicht vergessen, dass nur ein Teil dessen verschwunden ist, was an Grenzen existiert — viele unsichtbare Mauern zwischen uns bleiben immer stehen.

Seiichi Furuya, 1990

(Text für den Ausstellungskatalog »ZEICHEN im Fluß«, 1990: Museum des 20. Jahrhunderts Wien, Galerie Hlavního města Prahy, Muzej Suvremene Umjetnosti Zagreb, Pécsi Galéria)

Halbturn, 1981

Izu, 1978

1983 produzierte ich das Portfolio »Staatsgrenze 1981 – 1983, Teil I«, 23 mit kurzen Texten versehene Fotografien sowie eine Landkarte, auf der die Orte verzeichnet waren, an denen ich sie aufgenommen hatte. »Teil I« nannte ich die Arbeit deshalb, weil ich beabsichtigte, ihr schon bald einen zweiten Teil folgen zu lassen — eine Fotoserie von den Grenzen zu den anderen, nicht zum Ostblock gehörenden Nachbarländern Österreichs. Im Frühjahr 1984 wurde allerdings ein plötzlicher Umzug nach Dresden notwendig, und etwa um dieselbe Zeit wurde meine Familiensituation so schwierig, dass ich meine künstlerischen Aktivitäten ganz zurückstellen musste. So ist »Teil II« nie entstanden.

Anlässlich meiner Einzelausstellung im Heidelberger Kunstverein (»Wo die Wahrheit liegt«, 2014) wurde beschlossen, die Arbeit als Buch zu publizieren: »Staatsgrenze 1981 – 1983«. Seit der Produktion des Portfolios sind nun dreißig Jahre vergangen, eine Zeit, in der sich die Lage an den Grenzen dramatisch verändert hat. Einige Länder sind von der Landkarte verschwunden, andere neu hinzugekommen. Also begann ich, das Material von damals neu zu sichten — aus heutiger Perspektive und mit dem Bewusstsein des historischen Wandels, der seither stattgefunden hat. Das führte zur Erweiterung der ursprünglich 23-teiligen Arbeit um weitere sechs Fotografien, sodass das Buch nun die Grenzgeschichten von 29 Schauplätzen enthält.

Das Staatsgrenze-Projekt ging von einer sehr einfachen Frage aus, die sich nach meinem Umzug nach Mitteleuropa allmählich bei mir einstellte. Aus einem Land kommend, das keine künstlich gezogene Staatsgrenze besitzt, konnte ich mir nicht vorstellen, wie sich eine Grenze in der Landschaft physisch äußert. Das entscheidende Erlebnis hatte ich, als ich einmal an der Grenze zwischen Österreich und Jugoslawien fotografierte. Ich blickte immer wieder zwischen der mitgebrachten Landkarte und den sich vor mir ausbreitenden Weizenfeldern hin- und her, bis mir plötzlich klar wurde, dass das zu meinen Füßen fließende Rinnsal die Grenze war. Das eigenartige, mit Enttäuschung gepaarte Erfolgsgefühl werde ich nie vergessen.

Es ist nun vierzig Jahre her, dass ich Japan verließ und die Ozeangrenze des Pazifik und des japanischen Meeres überquerte.

Seiichi Furuya, 2013

1
1983年7月、不法越境を試みた4人のトルコ人がユーゴスラヴィア国境警備兵に射撃され、そのうちの1人が負傷した。最近、多くのトルコ人が「緑の国境」を越えオーストリア経由でドイツに辿り着こうとする。
ヴルツェン峠 1983

2
「国家社会主義者による暴政時代、マウトハウゼン強制収容所に監禁されていた囚人のうち数千人は——そのほとんどがフランス人——1943年から1945年の間、ロイブル峠トンネル建設工事に駆り出された。彼らの多くは非人道的な強制労働が原因で亡くなった」
（碑文より）
ローイブルパス 1983

3
連合赤軍テロリスト指名手配ポスター
セーベルグサッテル 1983

4
「垂れ幕には『神に仕えて25年』とスロベニア語で書いてあります。なぜなら、この地区の人々はスロベニア語をよりよく理解するからです」
グロバスニッツ 1983

5
「とんでもない！こっちにきてはだめ！こちらはユーゴスラヴィア、もし国境警備兵が巡回してきたら連行されるよ！」
スードスタイリッシェ・ヴァインシュトラーセ 1983

6
国境身分照会
シュピールフェルト 1983

7
ユーゴスラヴィア国内における食糧事情の悪化に伴い、ウイーン密輸徒党の活動が活発化した。1983年初頭、300キロあまりの密輸用挽き豆コーヒーを積んだゴムボードがラドカースブルグ近くのムーア河で転覆した。
ラドカースブルク 1983

8
「もしも貴方が3回大声で叫んだら、助けにきますよ」
ラッタースドルフ 1981

9
「水浴日和には、ハンガリー国境警備兵が望遠鏡を日光浴芝生に向けたまましばらく眺め続けているわ」
ロイパースバッハ・イム・ブルゲンラント 1981

10
「この鉄道路線を使って時々東欧からオーストリアに逃亡してくる人たちがいる。4年前には東ドイツの少女が西ドイツへ行く目的で不法越境してきた」
ロイパースバッハ・イム・ブルゲンラント 1981

11
「ここで西欧自由世界が終わり、そして再び日本で始まる。夜中に野生動物が国境線を跨ぐと照明弾が撃ちあがり、ハンガリー兵士が出動する」
シャッテンドルフ 1981

12
「ここにハンガリー軍のミグ21戦闘機が墜落した。日ならずしてハンガリー当局は機体残骸をすべて回収し同時にパイロットを連れ去った」
アンダウ 1981

13
合法越境者
ドイチュ・ヤールンドルフ 1981

14
1980年、22歳のチェコ人、ヅルバチェ・ミランは洪水状態のマルヒ河を泳いで渡ろうとした。彼の試みは死と引き換えに成功した。
マルヒエック 1981

15
1982年7月4日、ポーランド難民の農業飛行士と妻、娘の3人が乗るヘリコプターがウイーン郊外に着陸した。悪天候とチェコ国境縦断時の超低空飛行が彼等の亡命を成功させた。
ランゲンツァースドルフ 1982

16
「近年、鉄道路線ブレツラウフ—ウイーンの貨物列車を使って11人の東欧人がオーストリアに逃亡してきた」
ドレジング 1983

17
国境河川マルヒ
ホーエナウ 1983

18
「想像つくかね。1938年以前、8000人の住民のうち500人がユダヤ人だったんだ。（ニコルスブルク／ミクロフ）ユダヤ人は全て手中に収めていたのさ。幸いなことに「総統」の到来となって、彼等は消え去った。しかし結果的には我々はその街そのものを失ってしまった」
ドラーゼンホーフェン 1983

19
「4週間前、夜9時にたったパンツ1枚でパスポートをもったポーランド人がずぶ濡れ姿で玄関前に立っていた。彼は、ターヤ川を泳いで渡ってきて近くの天然ガスフレアを目指したと話した。すでに私たちは絶えまない発砲音を聞いていた。深夜を過ぎる頃まで国境は明るく照明されていた。彼は私たちの家でシャワーを浴び食事をとった。彼に着るものを与えてからラー・アン・デア・ターヤの地方警察を呼んだ」
ヴィルデンデュルンバッハ 1983

20
国境検問所
クラインハウグスドルフ 1983

21
「私はジプシーです。私たちの故郷は向こう側にあります。もう38年も経ってしまいました。そう、1945年、私たちは着の身着のまま、わずかな手荷物とともに立ち退かされました。オーストリア国内に留まることが出来なくてドイツへ行きました。私は故郷の事を一時も忘れたことがありませんし、ましてやどんな風にしてそこを去らねばならなかったも」
ウンターレッツバッハ 1983

22
「ヒットラーがオープンカーでツナイムからこの橋を渡ってきた時、私はまだ子供だった。反対側の丘には大きなハーケンクロイツの垂れ幕が張られ、我々子供たちはハーケンクロイツの小旗を振って彼を歓迎した。ドプチェック時代の1968年、この橋は再度国境の橋として使用されることになった。当時、オーストリアは橋の半分を緑色に、チェコは半分をグレーに塗装した。しかし、その1年後、ドプチェックが失脚すると戦車がやってきて橋の車道面を撤去してしまった。それ以来再びとても静かになった」
ハルデック 1983

23
国境線に沿ってパトロール飛行をするチェコ軍ヘリコプター
フラートレス 1983

24
「昨年の夏の終わり頃、当地の警官がキノコ狩りで国境を越えてチェコ側に入ってしまい逮捕された。年齢と性別や職業によって拘束期間が長かったり短かったりする。彼は2日後に釈放された」
カウツェン 1983

25
オーストリア最北端地点
ロートタール 1983

26
「4年前にチェコ人が潜水服を使って湖を潜りオーストリアに逃亡してきた。この事件以後チェコ当局は湖中に網を張りめぐらした」
シュタンカウアー・タイヒ 1983

27
「ここはまさにオーストリアのベルリンだ。三重の国境柵が市街を貫通していて、向こう側に住む人たちは別の政治統括のもとに暮らしている。正直言って、こちら側のほうがいいね」
グミュント 1983

28
「4年前に新しくこの関税局事務所が建てられた。当時多くの鳥が毎日このガラス窓に飛び込んで死んでしまった。我々は自然保護協会に問い合わせをして、確かスイスからだったと思うが、ステッカーを手に入れた。それ以来鳥が死ぬこともなくなった」
ヴァイゲチュラーク 1983

29
国境山岳ベーマーの森
クラファー・アム・ホッホフィヒト 1983

国境 1981－1983

オーストリアは７ヶ国の外国と国境を接している。
ドイツ連邦共和国、チェコスロバキア社会主義共和国、ハンガリー人民共和国、ユーゴスラビア社会主義連邦共和国、イタリア、スイス、リヒテンシュタイン公国とさまざまな政治基盤からなる国々、いわゆる東欧圏国、西欧自由主義圏国、中立国、公国など。

政治的な意図のもとに人為的に敷かれた境界線は人々にとって常に重要な役割を担ってきた。人類が存在する限りこの事実が変わることはないだろう。もし異星人に対峙して人類共同防衛なるものの必要性が生じた暁にはこれら国境はその重要性を失うだろう。

2706キロメートルに及ぶオーストリア国境は、たとえばコンクリート壁が一つの街そのものを無残にも二分割しているようなベルリンの壁と比べるとはるかに穏やかである。返ってそれは美しく、ロマンチックですらあり取り立てて目立つようなこともない。しかし、まさにこのような静かな風景のなかでこそひそやかな悲しい出来事の存在をベルリンよりも強く感じ取ることができる。

国境界隈を彷徨するなかで「国境」について考察する機会を己に課すべき意図のもとに、とくに悲しい出来事が起きた土地や場所を探したり、同時にほんの些細な個人的な物語に遭遇するようにと心がけた。

1983年　古屋誠一

国境 1981－1983

7年前、私は「国境 1981－1983」パートＩ（東欧ブロック諸国との国境）のプロジェクトを完了した。80年代末、モスクワを発生地とする「画期的、革命的」な台風が中央ヨーロッパを北から南に向かって通り過ぎた。現在この台風の目がちょうどバルカン辺りで停滞中といった状態だ。

オーストリアの「東欧ブロック」諸国に接する国境に関して言えば、第２次大戦後敷かれた政治的、非人道的なシンボルとして存在した国境は取りのぞかれた。悲劇の象徴としての国境は過去のものとなった。少なくとも可視的なバリケードは消失した。

今日「国境」のごとき作品の制作は不可能なものとなった。喜ばしいことにそれは歴史の一コマとなってしまった。しかし、消失したのは国境の一側面にすぎないことを、そして今もって目には見えない多くの壁が我々の間に存在することを忘れてはならない。

1990年　古屋誠一

1990年にウイーンの20世紀美術館で開催された展覧会"ZEICHEN im Fluß"（「浮游するシンボル」）のカタログ用のテキストとして書かれた。展覧会はプラハ市博物館、ザクレブ現代美術ギャラリー、ペーチ・ギャラリー（ハンガリー）に巡回した。

1983年、私は23点のテキストを添えた写真と撮影地名を記した地図からなるポートフォリオ「国境 1981－1983」パートＩを製作した。当時パートＩと副題を付けた理由は、パートIIとしていわゆる東欧ブロック諸国以外の国々とオーストリアの国境線を対象とした作品をやがて制作しようという意図があったからだ。しかし、1984年の春に急遽ドレスデンに一家で移住することとなり、また同時にその頃から家族を取り巻く環境も創作活動全般を制限せざるを得ないような緊迫したものとなり、結局パートIIは製作されず今日に至っている。

2014年にハイデルベルガー・クンストフェライン（Heidelberger Kunstverein）で開催される個展「真実のあるところ」の展示作品の一部として「国境」が選ばれ、同時に作品集「国境 1981－1983」を出版することが決まった。ポートフォリオを製作してから30年という歳月が流れ、この間に国境を取り巻く状況は激変した。ある国は消失し同時に新しい国が誕生した。作品集出版を契機に、これらの歴史的変動の事実を踏まえて「今日の視点」から当時の取材資料を再度見直すという作業を繰り返した。その結果、新たに6点の作品を、ポートフォリオに収めた23点に追加した。つまりこの作品集では29か所のそれぞれの国境物語が紹介されている。

国境線をもたない国に生まれ育った私が中央ヨーロッパに住むようになってから芽生えてきたごく単純な疑問から国境プロジェクトは始まった。当時の私には国境線が風景のなかで存在する形を具体的に想像することが出来なかった。印象深い体験をしたのは、ユーゴスラヴィアとオーストリアとの国境沿いを撮影した時だった。手元の地図と眼前に広がる麦畑を何度も見比べるうちに、まさに今私の足元に走る細流そのものが、探し求めていた国境線そのものであることに気付いた。その時の安堵と落胆の入り混じったような奇妙な感動を今でも忘れない。

太平洋、日本海と海の国境線を越えて私が日本国を去ってから今年で40年目を迎える。

2013年　古屋誠一

1
In July 1983, a Yugoslavian border patrol opened fire on four Turks crossing the border illegally. One of them was wounded. Presently many Turks are trying to cross the "green" border in order to reach Germany via Austria.
Wurzen Pass, 1983

2
"IN THE ERA OF NATIONAL-SOCIALIST TYRANNY, SEVERAL THOUSAND PRISONERS FROM THE CONCENTRATION CAMP MAUTHAUSEN—MOST OF THEM OF FRENCH NATIONALITY—WORKED ON THE LOIBL TUNNEL DURING THE YEARS 1943 TO 1945. MANY OF THEM DIED FROM THE BRUTAL FORCED LABOUR TO WHICH THEY WERE SUBJECTED."
(From the inscription on the memorial stone)
Loibl Pass, 1983

3
Wanted poster of RAF terrorists
Seebergsattel, 1983

4
"The poster reads '25 Years in the Service of God' in Slovenian, because the local community understands that better."
Globasnitz / Globasnica, 1983

5
"For God's sake, stay out! This is Yugoslavia. If the soldiers come along, they'll take you away!"
Südsteirische Weinstraße, 1983

6
Border control investigation
Spielfeld, 1983

7
The poor supply situation in Yugoslavia induced a Viennese smuggling ring to take action. At the beginning of 1983, a dinghy loaded with 300 kilograms of ground contraband coffee capsized on the Mur River near the town of Bad Radkersburg.
Radkersburg, 1983

8
"If you give three loud screams, I'll come and help you."
Rattersdorf, 1981

9
"On warm days fit for swimming, the Hungarian border guard spends a long time just watching our sun-bathing lawn through his telescope."
Loipersbach in Burgenland, 1981

10
"Sometimes people from the East flee to Austria on this railway line. Four years ago, a girl from East Germany crossed the border illegally in order to get to West Germany."
Loipersbach in Burgenland, 1981

11
"This is where the free Western world ends, and it only begins again in Japan. When wild animals cross the border strip at night, illuminating shells will flare and Hungarian soldiers come marching up."
Schattendorf, 1981

12
"This is where the Hungarian MiG-21 jet fighter crashed. The Hungarians soon came to collect all of the wreckage and pick up the pilot."
Andau, 1981

13
Legal border fliers
Deutsch Jahrndorf, 1981

14
In 1980, Dlubač Milan, a twenty-two-year-old Czech, attempted to swim across the swollen Morava River, which he succeeded in doing at the cost of his life.
Marchegg, 1981

15
On 4 July 1982, polish refugees—an agricultural pilot, his wife, and his daughter—landed near Vienna in a helicopter. A thunderstorm and low-altitude flying while crossing over the ČSSR made their adventure possible.
Langenzersdorf, 1982

16
"In recent years, eleven refugees from the East have entered Austria riding cargo trains on the tracks of the Břeclav–Vienna railway line."
Drösing, 1983

17
The Morava River as a border
Hohenau, 1981

18
"Can you imagine that 500 of the 8,000 local residents before 1938 were Jews (Nikolsburg / Mikulov). The Jews controlled everything. Thank God our Führer came and they disappeared! But then we lost the town ourselves."
Drasenhofen, 1983

19
"Four weeks ago at 9 p.m., a drenched Polish man appeared at our door dressed only in his underpants and carrying travel documents. He said he had crossed the Thaya River swimming and then followed the gas light near our natural-gas spring. We had already heard persistent shooting before that. The border was brightly lit up until after midnight. He had a shower and a meal at our place. We gave him clothes and called the constabulary in Laa an der Thaya."
Wildendürnbach, 1983

20
Border crossing
Kleinhaugsdorf, 1983

21
"I am a gypsy. Our home is over there. Thirty-eight years ago, yes, in 1945, we were expelled with no more than the clothes on our backs and a few bundles. We couldn't stay in Austria, so we went to Germany. I have never forgotten my home, nor how we left it."
Unterretzbach, 1983

22
"I was a little boy when Hitler came across this bridge from Znaim in a convertible. On the hill to the other side they had hoisted a giant swastika flag, and we children greeted him with our swastika flags. During the Dubček era, in 1968, the bridge was to be reopened as a border crossing. The Austrians painted their half of the bridge green, and the Czechs painted theirs grey. But one year later, after Dubček had been deposed, tanks came to dismantle the roadway. It has been very quiet again here since then."
Hardegg, 1983

23
The Czech military helicopter that patrols the border
Fratres, 1983

24
"Last year in late summer, a local police constable crossed the border onto Czech territory while he was collecting mushrooms. He was arrested. Depending on your age, sex, and profession, you can expect to be detained for either a short or a long period of time. He was handed back over after two days."
Kautzen, 1983

25
The northernmost tip of Austria
Rottall, 1983

26
"Four years ago, a Czech man in a wetsuit fled across the lake to Austria. After this incident, the Czech Republic installed a net all the way across the lake."
Stankauer Teich / Staňkovský rybník, 1983

27
"This is Berlin in Austria. The town is cut in half by a triple border fence, and the people on the other side live under a different political regime. Frankly, I prefer to be on this side."
Gmünd, 1983

28
"The new customs house was built here four years ago. Back then, many birds flew against the windows each day and were killed. We consulted a nature conservation association and got this sticker—from Switzerland, I think. There has been no problem since."
Weigetschlag, 1983

29
The Bohemian Forest border mountain range
Klaffer am Hochficht, 1983

Border 1981 – 1983

Austria borders on seven foreign countries:
the Federal Republic of Germany, Czechoslovakia, Hungary, Yugoslavia, Italy, Switzerland, and Liechtenstein—countries which represent the most diverse political systems: the so-called Eastern Bloc, one non-aligned state, the NATO, a neutral state, and a principality.

Artificially drawn political borders have always played an important role for mankind and probably will continue to do so as long as man exists. Such borders, I believe, will only lose their importance when common defence against an extraterrestrial enemy is called for.

The 1,681-mile-long Austrian border is far less brutal than, for example, the Berlin border, where a concrete wall cruelly cuts a city in half. It is even beautiful, romantic, inconspicuous, but in this quiet landscape one feels the silent, sad facts even more strongly than in Berlin.

On my trips along the border I have tried to find places where tragic incidents occurred and to dig up personal stories in my exploration of the "border" phenomenon.

Seiichi Furuya, 1983

Seven years ago I completed the project "Border Part I" (Border to the Eastern Bloc Countries). In the late 1980s, a "revolutionary" typhoon originating in Moscow had blown through Central Europe from north to south. From today's perspective, it looks as if the eye of the typhoon still hovers above the Balkans.

As far as the Austrian border to the "Eastern Bloc" is concerned, this symbol of political and human fates that emerged after the Second World War has been torn away. The border as fate is a thing of the past—the visible barriers have disappeared at any rate.

A work like "Border" would no longer be feasible today—it has already become history itself, which I find pleasing. But we must not forget that only one part of the existing borders have disappeared—many invisible walls always remain standing between us.

Seiichi Furuya, 1990

(Text for the exhibition catalogue "ZEICHEN im Fluß", 1990: Museum des 20. Jahrhunderts, Vienna; Galerie hlavního města Prahy, Prague; Muzej Suvremene Umjetnosti, Zagreb; Pécsi Galéria, Pécs)

In 1983, I compiled "Border 1981 – 1983, Part I", a portfolio of twenty-three photographs with accompanying text and a map of the locations I had photographed. The reason I added the subtitle "Part I" was because I intended to soon produce, as "Part II", a series of border photographs along the non-Eastern-Bloc countries neighbouring Austria. However, in the spring of 1984, my family and I moved to Dresden on short notice, and around the same time, my personal circumstances became very pressing, which forced me to restrict my artistic activities altogether. As a result, "Part II" never took form.

"Border" was chosen for inclusion in "Where the Truth Lies", a solo exhibition at the Heidelberger Kunstverein in 2014. It was also decided that we would publish a book, "Border 1981 – 1983". Some thirty years have passed since I created the portfolio, and during those years conditions around the borders have changed dramatically. Some countries have vanished, while others have been born. On the occasion of publishing the portfolio, I began a process of revisiting the materials from that time, from the perspective of the present, with an understanding of the historical changes that have taken place. This resulted in the addition of six photographs to the original twenty-three in the portfolio. In sum, this book presents the border stories of twenty-nine locations.

I began the border project with a very simple question that began to form when I moved to Central Europe after being born and raised in a country that had no man-made borderlines. At the time, I could not visualize how a national border would physically appear within a landscape. There was a crucial moment when I was photographing along the border between Austria and Yugoslavia. I kept looking at the map I was carrying and at the wheat fields spreading before me, when I realized that the stream flowing at my feet was itself the borderline I was searching for. I'll never forget the strange sensation of completion mixed with disappointment that I felt at that moment.

It has now been forty years since I left Japan, crossing the ocean borderlines of the Pacific and the Sea of Japan.

Seiichi Furuya, 2013

This insert is part of the artist's book "Border 1981 – 1983" by Seiichi Furuya and contains Japanese and English translations of the texts accompanying the photographic work, which Furuya originally wrote in German language. "Border 1981 – 1983" is a publication by the Heidelberger Kunstverein, Heidelberg, published by Spector Books, Leipzig, and the Izu Photo Museum, Shizuoka, in 2014.

境

Seiichi Furuya Staatsgrenze 1981 – 1983

Edited by Heidelberger Kunstverein

Concept Seiichi Furuya
Text Seiichi Furuya
Design Nicola Reiter
Typesetting Japanese Makoto Watanabe
Translation Michelle Dawn D'Atri, Seiichi Furuya,
John Junkerman, Wilfried Prantner
Printing Rema-Print_Littera Druck- u. Verlags GmbH, Wien

Published by
Spector Books, Harkortstrasse 10, D-04107 Leipzig
www.spectorbooks.com

and

Izu Photo Museum, Shizuoka, Japan
347-1 Clematis no oka, Higashino Nagaizumi-cho,
Shizuoka 411-0931 Japan
Tel.: +81(0)55-989-8780
www.izuphoto-museum.jp

Distributed in Japan by NOHARA

Thanks to Monika Faber (Photoinstitut Bonartes, Vienna), Galerie Thomas Fischer (Berlin), Koko Okano, Yoko Mori (Izu Photo Museum, Shizuoka), Maren Lübbke-Tidow (Camera Austria, Graz / Berlin), Susanne Weiß, Stefanie Kleinsorge (Heidelberger Kunstverein).

Spector Books: ISBN 978-3-944669-31-1
NOHARA: ISBN 978-4-904257-22-7

This publication was made possible thanks to the generous support of

ERSTE Stiftung BUNDESKANZLERAMT ÖSTERREICH